LORD, I WANT TO HAVE A QUIET TIME

Also by Carolyn Nystrom

Behold Your Lord: A Woman's Workshop on Jesus
At the Starting Line: Beginning a New Life
Characters and Kings: A Woman's Workshop on Israel under the Kings
People in Turmoil: A Woman's Workshop on 1 Corinthians
Before I Was Born
Angels and Me
New Life: A Woman's Workshop on Salvation
Jesus Is No Secret
Growing Jesus' Way
What Is the Bible?
A Woman's Workshop on David and His Psalms
A Woman's Workshop on Romans
A Woman's Workshop on James
What Happens When We Die?
What Is the Church?
What Is a Christian?
Why Do I Do Things Wrong?
What Is Prayer?
The Holy Spirit in Me
Who Is Jesus?
Who Is God?
James: Roadmap for Down-to-Earth Christians
Romans: Christianity on Trial
Acts: Church on the Move
Acts: Missions Accomplished
Mark: God on the Move
Forgive Me If I'm Frayed around the Edges

A ONE-YEAR PROGRAM

Lord, I Want to Have a Quiet Time

Learning to Study the Bible for Yourself

Carolyn Nystrom

Harold Shaw Publishers
Wheaton, Illinois

Copyright © 1984 by Carolyn Nystrom

Cover photo: Gary Irving

ISBN 0-87788-516-8

Library of Congress Cataloging in Publication Data
Nystrom Carolyn,
    Lord, I want to have a quiet time.

    Includes index.
    Summary: A guide for young adults in developing intimacy with God through Bible study during an established quiet time.
    1. Bible—Study.   [1. Bible—Study]   I. Title.
BS600.2.N95   1984   220'.07   84–13866
ISBN 0–87788–516–8

95 94 93 92 91 90 89 88 87 86   5 4 3 2

Contents

Before You Begin _____ 7

How to Use This Book _____ 8

1 Prayer: Talking & Listening _____ 9
Praise (Week 1) _____ 10
Petition (Week 2) _____ 13
Confession (Week 3) _____ 16
Intercession (Week 4) _____ 19
Thanksgiving (Week 5) _____ 21

2 How God Talks to Us _____ 24
Jesus Shows Us God's Will (Week 6) _____ 25
Encountering God (Week 7) _____ 27
Circumstances (Week 8) _____ 29
The Bible (Week 9) _____ 31

3 And the Walls Came Tumbling Down _____ 34
The Sin Barrier (Week 10) _____ 35
Jesus Breaks the Barrier (Week 11) _____ 37
Jesus, Our High Priest (Week 12) _____ 39

4 People Pens _____ 41
Cultural Differences (Week 13) _____ 42
The Body of Christ (Week 14) _____ 44
Economic Barriers (Week 15) _____ 47
Family Problems (Week 16) _____ 49
Personality Barriers (Week 17) _____ 51
Love Crumbles Barriers (Week 18) _____ 53

5 God: Continuous Creator _____ 55
First Creativity (Week 19) _____ 56
God Made Me (Week 20) _____ 58
Our Creative God (Week 21) _____ 60
New Creations in Christ (Week 22) _____ 65

6 Me: God's Creative Creature ———————————— 67
   God Makes Us Creative (Week 23) ———————— 68
   Creative Worship (Week 24) ————————————— 71
   A New Song (Week 25) ——————————————————— 76
   Creative Good Works (Week 26) ————————— 79

7 History's Hieroglyphics ———————————————— 82
   God Is Holy (Week 27) ————————————————— 84
   God's Covenant to Abraham (Week 28) ———— 86
   Escape (Week 29) ———————————————————————— 89
   The Promised Land (Week 30) ——————————— 91
   Punishment (Week 31) ————————————————— 93
   Back Home Again (Week 32) ——————————— 95
   Confident Worship (Week 33) ——————————— 98
   Practical Advice on Worship (Week 34) ————100
   Worship with the Psalms (Week 35) ——————102

8 Got the Message? Live It Out! ———————————106
   Faith during Hard Times (Week 36) —————————107
   Repentance (Week 37) —————————————————————111
   Freedom & Responsibility (Week 38) ——————114
   Reaching Out (Week 39) ————————————————————117

9 Beyond Mushroom Mentality ————————————————120
   A Bleak Future (Week 40) ———————————————————121
   The Comforter with Us (Week 41) ——————————124
   Supporting Each Other (Week 42) ——————————127
   A Glorious Future (Week 43) ——————————————131

10 On-your-own Bible Study ————————————————134
   Sample Study ————————————————————————————136
   John 11:1–44 (Week 44) ————————————————————142
   Weeks 45–52 ——————————————————————————————150

   Prayer Notebook ——————————————————————————151

   Scripture Index ——————————————————————————154

Before You Begin

"I'd like to have a quiet time, but I don't know what to do."

"I tried reading the Bible through, but I never could get past the laws of Leviticus."

"Sometimes I read the Bible, close it, and can't remember one idea. I might as well have been reading Swahili."

"I want to pray, but I don't know how to begin. So I just sit a while and wish I could think of something to say."

"I always intend to take time for Bible study and prayer, but I put it off, and then I forget. Pretty soon several days have gone by."

"Everybody says that Christians ought to have a quiet time. But why? Those quiet-time people make me feel guilty. But I also wonder if I'm missing something important."

Do any of the above statements have your name after them? If so, you have lots of company. Yet, God calls you and me to talk with him, to listen to him, to know him.

One of the greatest mysteries of the Christian faith is why the almighty, all-knowing, everywhere-present God desires us, mere flecks of his creation, to worship him. John 4:23 says that God seeks our worship. Why? I can only guess. But it would be foolish for us to reject this invitation to personal fellowship with God.

Perhaps this workbook studyguide will help your quiet time shape up. It gives references for Bible reading, questions to help you study the Bible references, and plenty of space for notes. Also included are ideas for prayer based on the passage you are studying and more space to make notes on what you are saying to God.

But if your quiet time ends when your prayer is finished and your Bible is closed, something basic is lacking. What God teaches you in your time alone with him should affect the way you think, what you do, and how you feel. Each study gives suggestions to help you think about the changes God would want you to make in your life.

How to Use This Book

The ten chapters of this book deal with major topics of the Christian life. Each chapter takes several weeks of study. If you complete the weekly studies on schedule, you will finish this workbook in a year. By then, you'll be well on your way to establishing good, consistent quiet-time habits. You will also have studied in detail a substantial portion of the Bible.

The first nine chapters of this studyguide provide forty-three weeks of five days each worth of questions to help you explore the passage at hand. These questions are designed to help you discover the content and meaning of the Scripture passages and to apply the truths learned to your life. Chapter ten shows you how to conduct your own inductive investigation of God's Word. For nine weeks, six days a week you will thoroughly examine passages of Scripture to come to an understanding on your own of what God intended to say in them and how you need to respond.

Before you begin, set a specific day of the week to start each new study topic. For example, you could begin a new topic every Monday. The first day read the entire weekly study—Scripture passage and all the questions—and mentally divide it over the week. Even if you cannot have a quiet time for a day or two, try to catch up and complete the study by week's end. If the Scripture passage is short, read it every day, making notes about new discoveries each time. A longer passage may be divided after the first day's reading and studied in parts.

Use a modern translation of the Bible. It will help clarify some of the language of the older versions. Try reading the Bible aloud as you study. Hearing, saying, and seeing the words simultaneously will help you remember them. And you'll soon know if your mind starts to wander—you'll stop hearing yourself read.

Be sure that your quiet time includes both Bible study and prayer. God wants to speak to you through his Word, but he also wants you to talk to him. Try praying aloud, too. You'll be amazed at how this helps you concentrate. Besides, prayer is more real in your own thinking if you've actually *said it.* You'll find the Prayer Notebook (pp. 151–155) helpful for keeping track of requests and answers as you intercede for yourself and others.

As this two-way communication with God grows, you will find yourself looking forward to your quiet time and feeling a void if you miss it. By then, you're on your way to making your quiet time a success.

1 Prayer: Talking & Listening

Elbows on closed Bible, I cried,
    Say, God, are you there?
    Knock, knock, I need you!
    Do you hear me?
    Talk to me.
    Tell me what to do.
    I've lost my way.
    I can't hear you.
        Say, God, are you there?
I waited for some flash of light,
A voice, a roar from God on high.
Instead I heard a gentle click,
    a door unlatched
    between the covers
    of his Book.

We talk to God. God talks to us. Communication between God and his people is two-way. During these first two months, you can learn about this two-way talk and practice some new ways of keeping the communication lines open.

The five studies in this chapter are about five kinds of prayer: praise, petition, confession, intercession, and thanksgiving. Just in case that all sounds very technical, take a look at the introduction to each study. You'll likely discover you're already using those prayers. But the Bible study should help you pray more as God intends.

The four studies in the next chapter deal with ways God talks to us. You might be surprised to discover that he's been talking to you all along. But maybe you'll find a few new ways to listen.

These Scripture study passages are short, but the questions have many answers. Read each passage several times during the week, and keep digging to find more answers. Fill up the pages with what God is teaching you.

Week 1 Praise

It's midterm exam time and you're burning the midnight oil to cram. By some fluke of fate, you're scheduled for your three toughest tests on the same day—tomorrow. It's enough to slay an Amazon. You've studied all you can, but history of civilization got shortchanged. You're pretty shaky on the overlapping influences of Egypt, Persia, and Greece. Another hour or two might clear it up, but you know your brain turns to sawdust on less than six hours of sleep. You hit the sack and turn it over to the Lord.

Next afternoon you trudge to history class to find that the exam is postponed. You whisper a quick prayer of *praise*, "God, you are wonderful, and I love you."

Read 1 Samuel 1:1–2:10, 21.

Day 1

1 Write what you think Hannah said when she prayed silently (1:13).

_____

_____

_____

_____

2 Read 1:8 and 1:18. What caused this change in Hannah?

_____

_____

Day 2

3 In what ways did Hannah show love for her son?

_____

_____

4 Hannah worshiped God with a prayer of praise. What did Hannah tell God of her feelings toward him (2:1)?

_____

_____

Day 3

5 How did she describe God? Begin each description with "God is . . ." (2:2–3).

_____

_____

_____

6 Find three contrasts in verses 4 and 5. What do these tell of God's character?

_____

_____

_____

_____

Day 4

7 List Hannah's account of God's actions (2:6–9).

_____

_____

_____

8 What does she say that God will do in the future (2:10)?

_____

_____

Day 5

9 Prayers of praise are like giving God a compliment. We tell him about the qualities of himself that we appreciate. On the next page make a list of good things God has done for you. Next to each item, write a "God is . . ." statement related to that gift. Today begin your prayer time with a note of praise from this list.

What God has done	*God is . . .*
Example: God gave me new friends when my best friend moved away.	God knows I need friends. He cares about the way I feel. God is a giver.

_____   _____

_____   _____

_____   _____

_____   _____

_____   _____

_____   _____

_____   _____

Week 2 Petition

You're coming home from a late meeting, and the road is far more slippery than when you left. It's hard to see through the snow. The car begins to swerve, and suddenly you see a telephone pole looming in front of you. You have time to gasp only, "Help, Lord!" A prayer of *petition*—in its simplest form.

Read Isaiah 36–37.

Day 1

1 What taunts did the Assyrian field commander use against the people of Judah (36:4–10)?

_____

_____

_____

2 How did the commander undercut the confidence of the people (36:11–20)?

_____

_____

_____

_____

Day 2

3 How did Hezekiah and his people respond to this threat from their enemy, Assyria (36:21–37:4)?

_____

_____

_____

4 What reassurance did the prophet Isaiah offer (37:5–7)?

_____

_____

Day 3

5 What did Hezekiah do with this new message from the king of Assyria (37:8–14)?

_____

6 What praise did Hezekiah offer God in his prayer (37:15–16)?

_____

7 What facts did he give God (37:18–19)?

_____

8 What did he ask God for (37:17, 20)?

_____

9 What reason did he give God for answering his prayer (37:20)?

_____

Day 4

10 What was God's response? (37:21–38)

_____

_____

Day 5

11 Bring a problem to God today. Write the facts on paper. Spread it before the Lord as Hezekiah did his letter. Date your request. Then leave a space to write how and when God answers your prayer.

Date:_____

Problem:_____

_____

_____

_____

_____

_____

_____

Answer:_____

_____

_____

Date:_____

Week 3 Confession

You blew it! It didn't seem so bad at the time, just a little lie and said with a smile. Someone might have even thought it was a joke. But it's mushroomed, and terrible consequences have resulted. Now you know it was all wrong from the beginning. You slip to your knees, bury your head in your arms, and *confess*, "God, I'm so sorry. I was wrong."

Read Luke 15:11-32.

Day 1

1 Why do you think the young man's plan looked good to him at first?

_____

_____

2 What went wrong?

_____

_____

Day 2

3 Study the young man's planned speech to his father in verses 17–19. What attitudes toward his father does this speech reflect?

_____

_____

_____

4 What attitudes toward himself and his actions?

_____

_____

Day 3

5 Do you think that the younger son's reception at home was more or less than he deserved? Why?

_____

_____

6 If you were given five minutes to defend the older brother's position, what points would you make?

_____

_____

_____

Day 4

7 If this story is a picture of God and his children when we sin, what does it reveal about the ingredients of confession?

_____

_____

About the way God responds to confession?

_____

_____

About the nature of forgiveness?

_____

_____

Day 5

8 Are you ever plagued by a vague feeling of guilt about all sort of things you've done in the past? God can heal those memories. Divide your past into three sections of time. One by one bring each section to God, confessing all your mistakes, failures, and sins of that time period. Trust him to enter your past and make you clean in his sight. Then read 1 John 1:9 to remind you of his forgiveness: "If we confess our sins, he is faithful and just, and will forgive our sins and cleanse us from all unrighteousness" (RSV).

Age 0–12_____

_____

_____

Age 12–15_____

_____

Age 15—present

Week 4 Intercession

Your best friend, Jim, is in an awful jam. His parents are getting a divorce. Neither wants him to live with them. His grades have hit the skids. He's quit coming to church and he says he might "drop out of life for awhile." You're not sure what he means by that, but you do know he needs more help than you can give. You pray, "God, help Jim . . ." And so you *intercede* for your friend.

Every Day
This week, pray for a different person or group each day. Use the prayers listed below and insert the names you have chosen in the prayers as you read them to God.

Prayer	*Name*
Hebrews 13:20–21	_____
1 Thessalonians 5:23	_____
Philemon 4–7	_____
Ephesians 3:15–21	_____
Romans 15:13	_____
2 Corinthians 13:7–9	_____

Read Genesis 13:1–13 and 18:16–33.

Day 1
1 Why did Abraham and Lot separate?

_____

_____

2 What reasons did Lot have for choosing the Sodom area?

_____

Day 2
3 Why did God tell Abraham that he was about to destroy Sodom?

_____

_____

_____

4 What attitudes did Abraham show when he spoke to God?

_____

_____

Day 3

5 What reasons did he give God for answering his request?

_____

_____

6 Was Abraham interceding for Sodom or for his nephew Lot?

_____

Day 4

7 What examples of Abraham's can you follow when you pray for someone else?

_____

_____

_____

_____

Day 5

8 What can you know of God from this passage?

_____

_____

_____

_____

Week 5 Thanksgiving

It's Saturday morning, bright, crisp, and clear. Autumn's skillful fingers have touched the fields and trees with gold. Even the air hints of gold dust suspended in sparkling liquid. You're free for the day—free in time and spirit. A morning walk in such milieu turns your mind to God who thought it all up even though you can hardly take it in. You whisper, "Thank you, my Lord."

Read Psalm 105, 106, 136.

Do not neglect to preview this week's entire study, since it may require more time than usual, and you will need to budget your schedule accordingly.

Day 1

1 All of these psalms praise God. Make notes about the characteristics of God that the psalmist appreciates.

Psalm 105:1–7 _____

_____

_____

_____

Psalm 106:1–5 _____

_____

_____

_____

Psalm 136 _____

_____

_____

_____

Day 2

2 Outline Psalm 105.

_____

_____

_____

_____

_____

_____

_____

3 How many times does the writer of Psalm 105 use the word *he* followed by a verb to show what God has done?

_____

Day 3

4 Why does the psalmist refer to God's steadfast love at the beginning and end of Psalm 106?

_____

5 What reason does the psalmist give God for saving his nation (106:47)?

_____

Day 4

6 Both Psalm 105 and 106 recount the history of Israel. How are their emphases different?

_____

_____

7 Which works of God are added in Psalm 106 to what the psalmist already gave thanks for in Psalm 105?

_____

_____

_____

Day 5

8 Each verse of Psalm 136 has the same refrain. What is it?

_____

9 Make a list on a separate sheet of paper of the works of God that make you thankful. Then think of a one-line refrain of praise. Write your own psalm of thanksgiving from this pattern.

My Psalm of Thanksgiving

_____

_____

_____

_____

_____

_____

_____

_____

_____

2 How God Talks to Us

Is prayer merely an exercise in self-dialogue, a handy way of sorting out our own thoughts? Did God give us the gift of prayer simply so that we could pretend that "somebody up there" cares about us?

No. God doesn't leave us to pray alone, our prayers bouncing back at us from off the ceiling. God is a God who hears us, who loves us, and who allows us the unspeakable privilege of knowing him.

God reveals himself in many ways. He doesn't expect us to stumble through life's choices in a vacuum, doing only what feels best at the time and hoping a God far away will understand. Instead he gives us guidelines for choices, and these guidelines are rooted in his own perfect nature.

During the next four weeks you'll study four ways that God communicates with us. They include: the person of Jesus Christ, a personal encounter with God himself, circumstances, and Scripture.

No one prays alone. God hears and returns the conversation.

Week 6 Jesus Shows Us God's Will

Have you ever wished for an older brother, one who would defend you, teach you, and introduce you to his friends? God talks to us in lots of ways. One of these is through the greatest older Brother ever—Jesus.

Read Hebrews 1.

Day 1

1 How does God speak to us differently from the way he did to his people of Old Testament times?

_____

2 List everything this passage says about God's Son.

_____

_____

_____

_____

_____

Day 2

3 What can you know about angels from this chapter?

_____

_____

_____

4 How is Jesus superior to angels?

_____

_____

_____

Day 3

5 How does this passage show that Jesus is also God?

_____

_____

_____

_____

6 What does the life of Jesus tell you about the nature of God?

_____

_____

_____

Day 4

7 What have you learned from the teachings of Jesus?

_____

_____

_____

Day 5

8 Read Romans 8:29. In what ways can you see that God is making you more like his first-born?

_____

_____

_____

9 List your activities for the coming week. What are some specific ways in which you can be more like Christ as you participate in these events?

_____

_____

_____

_____

Week 7 Encountering God

Do you ever wish that God would just sit down next to you and talk to you face-to-face as he did to Moses, Elijah, and the prophets? Then there would be no misunderstanding about whether God is leading you or your own thoughts are just adding to your confusion. God doesn't talk to us out loud now. Instead, the Holy Spirit lives inside us to help us know him. But he is the same God as in Old Testament times, and we can understand something of how he communicates with us by looking at how he talked to his people long ago.

Every Day

Sometimes we have to be quiet to understand what God is saying to us. This week, spend some of your devotional time each day being quiet before God. Empty your mind of other thoughts and concentrate on him. Let God reassure you of his presence. Let him bring understanding to what you have studied of his Word. Let him teach you to worship him.

Read 1 Kings 19.

Day 1

1 Why was Jezebel angry at Elijah? (For details see 1 Kings 18.)

_____

_____

2 Why was Elijah discouraged?

_____

_____

_____

Day 2

3 How did God strengthen and protect Elijah?

_____

_____

4 How did God encourage him?

_____

_____

Day 3

5 How did God illustrate his presence?

_____

_____

6 Which way did God choose to show himself to Elijah? Why do you think Elijah needed to know God in this way?

_____

_____

_____

Day 4

7 What did God tell Elijah?

_____

_____

8 How did Elijah change after meeting God?

_____

_____

Day 5

9 What do verses 11 and 12 teach about the ways God speaks to his people?

_____

_____

_____

10 Which way do you need to hear God speak? Why?

_____

_____

_____

Week 8 Circumstances

Do you sometimes look up after a long seige of things going wrong and wonder, "Is God trying to tell me something?" Or when everything is going great, do you say, "God must be with me"? Circumstances are not always an indication of God's leading, but they are one way that God helps us to know his will. Let's see how God used circumstances in Gideon's life.

Read Judges 6–7.

Day 1

1 Why were the Midianites giving the Israelites so much trouble?

_____

2 What reasons did Gideon have to doubt the angel's words?

_____

3 What circumstances reassured Gideon (6:16–24)?

_____

Day 2

4 What was God's first step to defeat the Midianites (6:25–35)?

_____

5 Describe Joshua's feelings. When have you felt like this?

_____

_____

Day 3

6 With all the enemies of Israel assembled at one spot, Gideon decided he needed even more evidence that God was with him. What signs did he receive this time (6:36–40)?

7 Why and how did God reduce Gideon's army from 32,000 to 300 (7:1–8)?

Day 4

8 What new circumstances did God use to convince Gideon that he was still on the right track (7:9–15)?

9 What results of this battle showed that God continued to be with Gideon (7:19–25)?

Day 5

10 Circumstances are not ironclad indications of God's will. But God's expectations of us are reasonable. He doesn't usually lead a D student to become a doctor. And he isn't likely to lead a gifted musician to stop his or her piano lessons. Today, list areas in which you have been successful. Make another list of areas in which you have had consistent failure. Present both lists to God, and ask his guidance in where you should concentrate your efforts.

Successes   *Failures*

Week 9 The Bible

And now for the most reliable method of all by which God communicates with us: the Bible. This week study what the Bible has to say about itself. Each day read a different passage and answer the questions for that passage.

Day 1

Read Psalm 1.

1 How does the writer of this passage feel about God's Word?

_____

2 What responsibilities does the reader of God's Word have?

_____

3 What blessings can one who studies and obeys God's Word expect?

_____

_____

4 If you believe and act on the teachings of this passage, what changes will you need to make?

_____

_____

Day 2

Read 2 Timothy 3:16–17.

1 How does the writer of this passage feel about God's Word?

_____

2 What powers does God's Word possess?

_____

_____

3 What responsibilities does the reader of God's Word have?

_____

4 What blessings can one who studies and obeys God's Word expect?

_____

5 If you believe and act on the teachings of this passage, what changes will you need to make?

_____

_____

Day 3

Read Psalm 19:7–14.

1 How does the writer of this passage feel about God's Word?

_____

2 What powers does God's Word possess?

_____

_____

3 What responsibilities does the reader of God's Word have?

_____

_____

4 What blessings can one who studies and obeys God's Word expect?

_____

_____

5 If you believe and act on the teachings of this passage, what changes will you need to make?

_____

_____

Day 4

Read Hebrews 4:12.

1 How does the writer of this passage feel about God's Word?

_____

2 What powers does God's Word possess?

_____

3 What responsibilities does the reader of God's Word have?

4 What blessings can one who studies and obeys God's Word expect?

5 If you believe and act on the teachings of this passage, what changes will you need to make?

Day 5

Read Psalm 119:97–112.

1 How does the writer of this passage feel about God's Word?

2 What powers does God's Word possess?

3 What responsibilities does the reader of God's Word have?

4 What blessings can one who studies and obeys God's Word expect?

5 If you believe and act on the teachings of this passage, what changes will you need to make?

6 God will never, never, never lead you to do something that is against the teachings of Scripture—not by circumstances, not by an inner feeling, not by the advice of your friends. What plan of action can you form to show God that you care about what he has to say to you through his Book?

3 And the Walls Came Tumbling Down

Once
there was a barrier between
  God and man.
  Jesus ripped it
  top to bottom
and thus he trampled
  underfoot
the walls men build
between themselves.

Walls. We build them. We stumble over them. We hide behind them. They become our prisons. And God doesn't want his people behind bars. Each Scripture passage in this chapter and the next speaks of walls. Read the passage and questions for the week several times. Schedule your time to complete all the questions within the week. Study. Think through the questions. Most of the questions have several answers. See if you can find a few new ideas to record each time you read.

Pray. Ask God to reveal any barriers between himself and you. Unconfessed sin can bring coldness to your fellowship with God. So can an unwillingness to obey him.

Then review your contacts with other people. Ask God to point out walls between you and them. (It doesn't matter who built the walls.) Pray for those people on the other side. Then seek his help in bringing the barriers to a crashing end.

Week 10 The Sin Barrier

You've just returned from a noisy outdoor concert. Your ears are still ringing from the sound. Your hair smells like a burnt rope. You've heard so many obscenities from the crowd in the past two hours that they sound almost natural. On the way home, you flip on the radio and catch a newscast full of rape, murder, and war. You wonder, "How can dirty, ugly, sinful mankind approach a holy God?"

Read how God circumvented this barrier in the Old Testament.

Read Exodus 26:31–37 and Leviticus 16.

Day 1

1 Draw a picture of what is described in the Exodus passage.

2 What was the purpose of the veil?

Day 2

3 When and under what conditions was the high priest to enter the holy place within the veil (see Lev. 16)?

4 What reasons does God give for these restrictions?

Day 3

5 What was the purpose of the bull (16:11–14)?

_____

6 What was the purpose of the goat used for a sin offering (16:15–19)?

_____

7 What function did the scapegoat serve (16:20–22)?

_____

Day 4

8 How was the veil a barrier between God and man?

_____

_____

9 How was it also a link?

_____

_____

Day 5

10 What can you know about the nature of God from these passages?

_____

_____

_____

Pray, worshiping him for these qualities.

Week 11 Jesus Breaks the Barrier

Easter bunnies made of sugar; Easter clothes, more fancy than you like; Easter baskets—wicker, Easter marshmallow chickens, Easter baskets in the form of fire trucks and cowboy hats—for little boys, Easter cellophane grass; "Easter Parade" blaring from the loudspeaker. The department store is geared up for the next big holiday.

Somewhere you notice a cross, but even that is candy-coated, not at all resembling jagged wood and rugged spikes, anguish, blood, torturously slow death.

So Easter celebrates Christ's death and resurrection, or are they thinking only that God died?

Read Matthew 26–28.

Day 1

1 What indications are there that Jesus knew he would die (26:1–45)? List the verses as well.

_____

_____

_____

_____

2 What shows that this whole process was emotionally, spiritually, and physically painful to him (26:36–45)?

_____

_____

_____

Day 2

3 How is Christ's blood like the scapegoat of Leviticus 16?

_____

_____

4 What supernatural phenomena accompanied his death (27:50–54)?

_____

_____

5 In view of its Old Testament purpose and use, what is the significance of the torn temple veil? (See Exod. 26:31–37.)

_____

_____

Day 3

6 How is the relationship between God and man different because of Christ's death and resurrection?

_____

_____

_____

Day 4

7 What does it mean to you that you can, by prayer, come into the presence of a holy God through Jesus' name?

_____

_____

Day 5

8 What do you know of Jesus from these chapters in Matthew?

_____

_____

_____

_____

Pray, thanking God for these characteristics.

Week 12 Jesus, Our High Priest

"And finally, beloved congregation . . ." You sigh as Pastor winds up his message. You have been daydreaming during the sermon in spite of your best intentions. You straighten your back, determined to at least tune in now. And so you hear the end of what must have been a substantial message: "We see Christ, the Great High Priest, taking the place of the entire old system of priesthood and at the same time becoming the blood sacrifice necessary for an atonement of sin—not just for one year but for all men and forever. The shredded temple veil leaves naked before us the Mercy Seat, where we can come face-to-face with a holy God. Though we may cover our own eyes in shame because of our sin, God receives us in love through his Son."

Read Hebrews 7:22–10:25.

Day 1

1 How is Jesus like the Old Testament high priests?

_____

2 How is he different?

_____

_____

_____

3 List the promises of the new covenant (8:10–12).

_____

_____

_____

Day 2

4 What does it mean to you to know that God says, "I will be your God"?

_____

_____

_____

5 In what ways was the holiness of God emphasized by the Old Testament method of sacrifice (9:1-10)?

_____

_____

6 What did it cost Jesus to become the High Priest forever (9:11–15)?

_____

Day 3

7 Have you accepted Christ's gift that breaks down the wall between you and God and offers permanent forgiveness for your sins?

   If yes, thank him again for this gift.

   If no, would you like to receive him?

   a. Confess to him that you have sinned.

   b. Tell him that you accept his gift of new life now.

   c. Promise that you will try as hard as you can, with his help, to obey him in everything.

   d. Christ has already promised to receive you (John 6:37).

Day 4

8 What does God ask us to do as a result of Christ's work for us (10:19–25)?

_____

_____

_____

9 In which of these areas do you need to improve? What steps can you take to improve?

_____

_____

_____

Day 5

10 Who needs your encouragement this week?

_____

11 What will you do for him or her? When?

_____

_____

4 People Pens

Farm yards provide a graphic picture of separation. The goats graze in their own grass pasture, with a sturdy fence separating them from the yard. The fence keeps them from eating a pair of jeans off the line, which they like as much as grass.

Pigs wallow in their own pens placed down-wind from the farm house. (Pigs smell best in the form of bacon.)

The cows amble through their wide barb-wired meadow. They don't mix well with pigs and are apt to trample chickens.

And chickens? They peck away in a small enclosed dirt yard with chicken wire high enough to keep them from flying over and annoying any animal not equally airborne. Each animal in its own fenced-in area—a perfectly appropriate arrangement for farm animals.

And people, even God's people, may industriously build invisible pens around themselves: for protection, for convenience, for privacy, for safety. Their pens say, "My space is for me and my own kind—the rest of you stay out!"

But when Jesus, by his death, ripped the temple veil—a symbolic barrier between God and man—he also trampled underfoot the walls we build between ourselves. During the next six weeks you will look at six different settings where people try to isolate themselves. And six Scripture studies will encourage you to stay out of those "people pens."

Week 13 Cultural Differences

A letter arrives from unpredictable Aunt Sara, missionary to Indians in mountainous Colombia. She's coming home on furlough. This time there's a new wrinkle in her every-four-years' visit. She's bringing a family of Indians with her—mother, father, and four small children. She writes, "Don't worry about beds, they're all used to sleeping in one bed or hammock, whichever is available. Only plan two meals a day. We can't upset their digestive systems. Please try to have some coarse whole-grain foods. You may have to explain bathroom procedures. They've never used one before." (You eye the new carpet in your small apartment's living room.) "And by the way, they speak little English but are very receptive to the gospel in their own tongue." (You don't happen to speak their language.) "And don't worry," she adds, "we won't stay long." (Long? You don't know if you're even up for an overnight.)

Read Acts 10:1–11:26.

Day 1

1 What were the cross-cultural hurdles Peter had to make to go to Cornelius (10:9–14; 27–29)?

_____

_____

2 Why was Cornelius fertile ground for the gospel?

_____

_____

Day 2

3 What are the indications that Cornelius was willing to be taught by Peter?

_____

_____

4 What do you think made it possible for Peter, a Jew, and Cornelius, a Gentile, to talk and listen to each other?

_____

_____

Day 3

5 What information did Peter give Cornelius?

_____

_____

_____

_____

6 What do you think was his most important point? Why?

_____

_____

Day 4

7 When Peter defended his actions, what authority did he use?

_____

8 How did God use Barnabas to build on what Peter had learned?

_____

_____

Day 5

9 Maybe it's not primitive Indians on the other side of your barrier. But what about a foreign-born co-worker, or someone whose Christian doctrine is so different from yours that it hardly seems like the same faith? Or maybe your family is thinking of taking in a troubled foster child. Who is the "Cornelius" in your life?

_____

What can you do to show him that Jesus Christ is "Lord of all"?

_____

_____

_____

Week 14 The Body of Christ

"Mr. Moderator, I'd like to speak against the motion that we pay the church organist."

The organist is not present at the annual church business meeting, but his wife is. She sits motionless and looks straight ahead.

"I think it would set a precedent we don't want to follow. Sure, Matt is talented; we could never pay him what he's worth. But we have talented Sunday school teachers, and a talented librarian, and a talented superintendent. We even have a talented church treasurer. But we don't pay any of them—and we shouldn't. We shouldn't pay a church organist either."

The church business meeting staggers on. First one side and then the other addressing what at first appeared a minor issue. Before it is over, two families (one from each side) have resolved to leave the church.

And for the church, the model of Christian unity—so much so that Paul calls it "the body (singular) of Christ"—something has gone crazily awry.

Read Ephesians 4:1–16.

Day 1

1 Make a list of the ways in which we are "one" (4–6).

_____

_____

2 What gifts did Jesus give (8–11)?

_____

_____

3 For what purposes were the gifts given?

_____

_____

Day 2

4 Who does the "work of ministry" (12, RSV)?

_____

5 Why should we become spiritually mature (13–16)?

_____

_____

Day 3

6 From your own experience, give some examples of speaking the truth *without* love.

_____

_____

_____

Give some examples of speaking the truth *in* love.

_____

_____

_____

Day 4

7 How is your church acting like one body with Christ as the head?

_____

_____

8 What gifts (ability or service) should you contribute to this body?

_____

_____

9 How can you work toward overcoming barriers within your church?

_____

_____

_____

Day 5

10 Think of one person in your church with whom you do not work well (it might be someone much older or younger). Pray for this person.

This week, take one positive step toward working together as part of the body of Christ. What do you plan that step to be?

_____

_____

_____

Week 15 Economic Barriers

Where do you live, right side of the tracks or wrong? How about your race—majority or minority? When you choose friends, what do you look for? Probably you look for people mostly like yourself. It's easier to feel comfortable with them. But how do you feel about those who are of a different race, a different social status, those who can't match you dollar for dollar—or those whom you can't match? How do you treat them?

Read Philemon.

Day 1

1 Think of one person that verses 4–7 describe. Write the prayer using his or her name.

_____

_____

_____

_____

_____

_____

_____

_____

Now pray it.

Day 2

2 What were the social, class, and economic differences between Paul, Philemon, and Onesimus?

_____

_____

_____

Day 3

3 How had the status of Onesimus changed since he became a believer? How was it the same?

_____

_____

4 To what extent was Paul willing to go to bat for him?

_____

Day 4

5 What changes from the usual master-slave relationship was Paul requesting? (See also Eph.6:5–9.)

_____

_____

Day 5

6 Think of one Christian that you have trouble loving because of social, racial, or economic differences. What can you do to treat that person as a "beloved brother or sister"?

_____

_____

_____

_____

Week 16 Family Problems

There go Mr. and Mrs. Taylor. Their family is such a model their backyard fruit tree must grow homemade apple pie. Mrs. T. has a ready smile that's not phony. Mr. T. listens appreciatively to his wife, and a quick caress isn't unusual. Yet he speaks with authority when it's his turn. Paul T., age 12, is the only kid in church who isn't afraid to pray out loud in an adult prayer service. Lynn T., age 10, acts as if she really likes to look after Craig, who is 2. She plays with him constantly. When Craig takes turns sitting on laps, each family member acts like Craig is doing him a favor. Sue T., who is 16, has a Bible study at the high school, and lots of kids think the Bible is OK just because Sue is wonderful. A college student once said, "Just knowing the Taylors reassures me that it's possible to get married and have things work out right."

You know deep down that any family, even the Taylors, can't be perfect. But still there must be some system for making a family come off even passing good. How do they do it?

Read Ephesians 5:15–6:4 every day.

Day 1

1 What are four results of being filled with the Spirit (5:19–21)?

_____

_____

_____

2 Name specific ways in which each member of your family can be "subject to one another out of reverence for Christ."

_____

_____

_____

_____

Day 2

3 List the commands to a wife.

What reasons are given?

Day 3

4 List the commands to a husband and father.

What reasons are given?

Day 4

5 List the commands to children.

What reasons are given?

Day 5

6 Which member of your family is hardest for you to get along with?

What changes toward that person should you make in order to follow these commands?

Week 17 Personality Barriers

Ella is new at work. She is fat, ugly, has long, dark, stringy hair, talks loudly, and chews gum with her mouth open. Besides that, she doesn't practice "personal hygiene."

You know that Christ died for everyone, but surely he doesn't expect you to take someone like Ella under your wing. Why if she were a Christian, she wouldn't even give his cause a good image!

Read Mark 10:46–52; Luke 19:1–10; John 4:4–42.

Day 1

Try to answer the questions for each of the three main characters.

1 What made each one appear to be an unsuitable follower of Jesus Christ?

Bartimaeus?_____

_____

Zacchaeus?_____

_____

Woman of Samaria?_____

_____

2 What was the response to each of the people surrounding Jesus?

Bartimaeus?_____

_____

Zacchaeus?_____

_____

Woman of Samaria?_____

_____

Day 2

3 What are the indications that each wanted to know Christ?

Bartimaeus?_____

_____

Zacchaeus?_____

_____

Woman of Samaria?_____

_____

Day 3
4 How did Christ respond to each?

Bartimaeus?_____

_____

Zacchaeus?_____

_____

Woman of Samaria?_____

_____

Day 4
5 What evidence is there that each was useful to him?

Bartimaeus?_____

_____

Zacchaeus?_____

_____

Woman of Samaria?_____

_____

Day 5
6 Think of one person who is naturally repulsive to you. Pray for that person. What is one act that you can do to show that person that Christ cares for him or her, and that you do, too?

_____

_____

Try it.

Week 18 Love Crumbles Barriers

Lord God,

There's this guy at work I just can't stand. On a Monday morning he can saunter through the plant whistling gospel tunes. Last week he stood next to my machine and just talked—on and on. The guy must be blind not to notice that I was working my tail off to make the piece rate. The last thing I need is a gabber to mess up my rhythm. (Maybe he doesn't need the money, but I do.)

And he carries this big grin around with him all day long. All this "Happy Joe" stuff has got the other workers tapping their heads behind his back.

Lord, I know I'm supposed to love this guy. (He's my Christian brother.) But I don't even like him.

Read 1 John 3:11–4:21; John 13:34–35.

Day 1

1 In what ways does John tell us that God showed his love to us (1 John 4:9–11)?

_____

_____

2 What are some ways that we can imitate God's love in our relationships with others?

_____

_____

Day 2

3 What reasons are given for showing love to each other (John 13:35; 1 John 4:11–12)?

_____

_____

Day 3

4 What effect does the love of believers for each other have on nonbelievers (1 John 4:4–6; John 13:35)?

_____

_____

Day 4

5 First John 3:18 speaks of love as more than words (and feelings)—as deeds. What can you do to be loving toward someone even if you don't *feel* loving? Think about a specific person.

_____

_____

_____

Day 5

6 How does knowing that another Christian loves you make it easier for you to love God?

_____

_____

5 God: Continuous Creator

void, darkness
God spoke.
light, land, water,
seed, beasts
Yet God wouldn't rest.
dust, a rib
man, woman
in his image
Breath of life from God—
shaped in his image
Alive!
And God rested.

God rested—after his period of initial creation—but not for long. The Scripture is full of God's creative activity. Sure, he made the world and all that's in it. (That includes the stars, light years away and all those billions of stars beyond the ones we've discovered.) But when that was finished, God kept right on creating. He created people—not just the first two—but every tiny baby born since. David said in a prayer to God,

"For you created my inmost being;
you knit me together in my mother's womb" (Ps. 139:13, NIV).

The prophet Isaiah spins chapter after chapter, singing of God's overwhelming creative power. And the Apostle Paul talks about God creating new life in the inner being of all who receive Jesus Christ. So God may have rested—but not for long. He keeps right on creating, even now.

During the next four weeks you'll study Scriptures that speak of God's continuous creativity. And after each study you'll find a suggestion for your own creative worship of our creative God.

Week 19 First Creativity

Got an urge to create? Like to build, paint, write, sew, or sing? What causes you to read a story and think how you would have ended it differently? How do you think up new games to entertain the little kid next door? What makes you rearrange a room until the whole setting is one that says, "Now it's finally right (at least for this week)"? God started it way back "in the beginning."

Read Genesis 1–2.

Day 1

1 What words and phrases are repeated? Make a list.

_____

_____

_____

2 What do these tell you about God?

_____

_____

Day 2

3 What words would you use to describe God's creativity?

_____

_____

4 How did God show that he cared about man?

_____

_____

Day 3

5 In what ways did God make men and women different from the rest of his creation?

_____

_____

6 What difference does it make to you that you are created in God's image?

_____

_____

_____

Day 4

7 What do you need to change in order for your creativity to be more like the creativity of God?

_____

_____

8 Now tell God about this in a written prayer.

_____

_____

_____

_____

Day 5

9 Read all of Genesis 1–2 again today. Meditate on the character of God as it is revealed in these chapters. Praise him, in prayer, for these qualities.

Week 20 God Made Me

Ever feel like an unimportant blob in the midst of a vast universe, as if what you say and think doesn't matter? Maybe our whole world doesn't matter. It's just a "fleck of sand" anyway. Ever wonder if it makes any difference what you do or whether you exist at all? Will anyone know, or care, in a hundred years? Let's see it from God's perspective.

Read Psalm 139 every day.

Day 1

1 How does the psalmist describe God's knowledge?

_____

_____

2 List the places the psalmist says you could expect to find God.

_____

_____

Day 2

3 What does God know about you?

_____

_____

4 When did God begin to care about you?

_____

Day 3

5 God created a special gift of yourself for you. How can this change the way you feel about yourself?

_____

_____

Day 4

6 Make a list of your characteristics, abilities, and personality traits.

_____

_____

_____

_____

_____

Thank God for each one of these, and ask his help in using this creation of yourself to please him.

Day 5

7 Psalm 139 is a beautiful prayer. It includes praise, worship, and much of the psalmist's inner feelings, as well as requests. Today write a prayer that has these elements. Then pray it to God.

_____

_____

_____

_____

_____

_____

_____

_____

_____

_____

_____

_____

Week 21 Our Creative God

What is God like? What does he do? Who is he? How can you describe God? What does your mind see when you say the word *God*? A God who created everything you know of is a pretty big God. Part of worship is recognizing God's characteristics and praising him for them. Biblical writers tried to describe God's creativity. Read one of the five listed chapters each day. Then write answers for that chapter.

Every Day

Page through a hymnal or songbook. Find a song that says what you would like to tell God. Then sing it to him each day this week.

Day 1

Read Psalm 104.

1 What do the word pictures of verses 1–4 contribute to your feelings about God?

_____

_____

2 How do verses 5–9 help you see God's orderliness in something as devastating as the flood?

_____

_____

_____

3 According to verses 10–26, what all has God made?

_____

_____

_____

_____

4 Why can the psalmist say in verse 24, "In wisdom you made them all"?

_____

_____

5 Notice the words in verse 27, "These all look to you." In what ways do verses 27–30 illustrate God's continuing creation?

_____

_____

_____

6 Is your response to this psalm's description of God similar to verses 31–35? If so, read it as your prayer of praise to God.

_____

Day 2

Read Isaiah 42

7 Verses 1–4 foretell the coming of Jesus. What do they reveal about his work?

_____

_____

8 How can a belief in God as Creator keep us from idolatry (5–9)?

_____

_____

9 What reasons do verses 10–17 show you for joining in the praise written here?

_____

_____

10 What steps did God take in verses 18–25 to keep his people from being blind and deaf to him?

_____

_____

_____

11 Find one verse from Isaiah 42 that tells how great God is. Write it down.

_____

_____

_____

Day 3

Read Isaiah 43.

12 Which verses refer to God as Creator?

_____

13 What do they say he created?

_____

_____

14 What motivation do you find here to not value anyone or anything more than God?

_____

_____

15 Find one verse from Isaiah 43 that tells how great God is. Write it here.

_____

_____

_____

Day 4

Read Isaiah 44.

16 From verses 1–5, what can you know of God's continuing creation?

_____

_____

17 Verses 6–23 are often referred to as one of the strongest statements against idolatry in all of Scripture. What do you find here that would turn you from other gods?

_____

_____

_____

18 What do you find in the same verses that would turn your worship to the one true God?

_____

_____

19 How might God's ability to create (and re-create) inspire you to worship?

_____

_____

20 Find one verse from Isaiah 44 that tells how great God is. Write it here.

_____

_____

_____

Day 5

Read Isaiah 45.

21 What different forms does God's creative power take in this chapter?

_____

_____

_____

22 Verses 9–13 begin with the words, "Woe to him who quarrels with his Maker." What reasons do these verses give for not quarreling with God?

_____

_____

23 Find as many repetitions as you can of the refrain, "I am the LORD and there is no other." What all does God compare himself to in order to show that he alone is God?

_____

_____

_____

24 Verse 22 says, "Turn to me and be saved." Why might you want to turn to God as he is described in this chapter?

_____

_____

25 What would you hope this creative God would create in you?

_____

_____

26 Find one verse from Isaiah 45 that tells how great God is. Write it here.

_____

_____

_____

Week 22 New Creations in Christ

When God planned you, even before you were born, he knew that you would never be able to measure up to his standards. He knew that you would be subject to temper tantrums, feelings of jealousy, disobedience, selfishness, and all kinds of other sins. Therefore, he planned a way to make you new on the inside. Christ died for us, but his creative work on our behalf didn't end; it was only beginning. By his Spirit, he is continually making us beautiful new creations in his own image.

Every Day

Many of the people you see every day are in slavery to sin. Some would like to have the freedom of forgiveness and new life in Christ. God may already be preparing them to receive his free gift. Ask God to bring these people to your attention. This week pray each day for one of your acquaintances who does not know Christ. Some time during the week, worship God by presenting the gospel to that person. Write his or her name here:

_____

Read Romans 6.

Day 1

1 In what ways has Christ made it possible for us to be like him (1–11)?

_____

_____

Day 2

2 What responsibilities do we have for our bodies (12–14)?

_____

_____

Day 3

3 Contrast the effects of slavery to sin with the results of slavery to God. Make a list for each.

Slavery to Sin   *Slavery to God*

_____   _____

_____   _____

_____   _____

4 According to verse 23, what is the final result of each kind of slavery?

_____

Day 4
5 Write some specific effects of your sin.

_____

_____

Day 5
6 Write specific effects of your acts of obedience to God.

_____

_____

7 Which kind of slavery do you prefer? Why?

_____

_____

_____

6 Me: God's Creative Creature

How can we, human beings created by God and created again with new life in Christ, respond to this creative God—our Maker? Creatively, of course.

Here too, Scripture gives us guidelines on how and when, and with what kind of help. The next four weeks' study outlines some of these ways.

First, part of new life in Christ grants us the indwelling presence of God the Holy Spirit. So we don't have to worry about whether our creative genes are as powerful as those of the next person. God created us the way he chose. And through the power of his Holy Spirit, we too can create.

But create how? Many, many ways. But we'll look at three. We can worship God through creative use of our bodies, we can worship him through music, we can worship through work. And our God who loves creativity receives it all.

Week 23 God Makes Us Creative

When you look inside yourself, what do you see? No, not the X-ray, CAT scan version of bone, muscle, tendon. But what do you see of the inner you? The motives, feelings, thoughts, plans, desires. Ever wish you could turn the secret you inside out and send it to the cleaners?

God's offer of new life isn't just a paper promise. He offers to be that cleaner for you. God never says, "You clean up your life and then you may come to me." He says, "Come, I'll help with the bath."

This week, you'll study four Scriptures that will help you become more and more that new creation God envisioned of you when you first gave yourself to Jesus.

Every Day

As part of your creative worship this week, select a psalm that expresses what you feel. Write it in the space below. Then each day use it as a prayer.

_____

_____

_____

_____

_____

_____

_____

_____

_____

_____

_____

_____

_____

_____

_____

_____

Day 1

Read 1 Samuel 9:25–10:13.

1 What signs did Samuel give Saul that God was working?

_____

_____

_____

2 What did God do for Saul?

_____

Day 2

Read John 14:15–31.

3 What does Jesus promise us if we love him?

_____

_____

4 What does he expect from us?

_____

_____

5 How can you make yourself a better "home" (23) for God?

_____

_____

_____

Day 3

Read 2 Corinthians 5:14–21.

6 What does it mean to be a new creation in Christ?

_____

_____

_____

_____

Day 4

Read Ephesians 4:17–32 today and tomorrow.

7 Make a list of the contrasts between the old nature and the new nature.

Old Nature   *New Nature*

_____   _____

_____   _____

_____   _____

Day 5

8 How is God making you new? Make notes of some of these inside changes.

_____

_____

Thank God for these, and then ask him for help in specific areas that still need cleansing.

_____

_____

Week 24 Creative Worship

God created our bodies, each one differently. We can use these bodies to express worship. Sometimes we pray with folded hands, as if placing them between his in commitment. We may bow our heads in submission or lift them to give attention to him. We may open our hands palms up to receive from him or to release ourselves to him. We can lift our hands, as if reaching toward God in worship.

Confession of sins seems more real if we kneel before him, a mighty and holy Lord. We cause our lips to speak to him and of him. We discipline our minds and spirits to think of him when we read his Word and pray. This week's Scripture passages speak of worshiping God with our bodies.

Every Day

Concentrate on prayer this week. As you pray, let your body reflect the words of your prayers. Give your body as a living sacrifice to God (Rom. 12:1), and use it to worship him.

Day 1

Read Romans 12:1–3.

Each day this week, read the suggested passage for the day. Then respond to the questions below with information and thoughts gleaned from that passage.

1 Find as many references as you can to the body, its parts or position. How are these used in prayer or worship?

Body Part	Refer-ence	How Used

2 What characteristics of God inspire each of these gestures of worship?

_____

_____

_____

_____

_____

3 Romans 12:1–3 speaks of the body and the mind. How can your body aid your mind in worship?

_____

_____

_____

_____

_____

Day 2

Read 1 Timothy 2:1–8.

1 Find as many references as you can to the body, its parts or position. How are these used in prayer or worship?

Body Part	Reference	How Used
_____	_____	_____
_____	_____	_____
_____	_____	_____
_____	_____	_____

2 What characteristics of God inspire each of these gestures of worship?

_____

_____

_____

_____

_____

3 Romans 12:1–3 speaks of the body and the mind. How can your body aid your mind in worship?

_____

_____

_____

_____

_____

Day 3

Read Psalm 63.

1 Find as many references as you can to the body, its parts or position. How are these used in prayer or worship?

Body Part	Refer- ence	How Used
_____	_____	_____
_____	_____	_____
_____	_____	_____
_____	_____	_____
_____	_____	_____

2 What characteristics of God inspire each of these gestures of worship?

_____

_____

_____

_____

3 Romans 12:1–3 speaks of the body and the mind. How can your body aid your mind in worship?

_____

_____

_____

_____

Day 4

Read Psalm 95.

1 Find as many references as you can to the body, its parts or position. How are these used in prayer or worship?

Body Part	Refer-ence	How Used
_____	_____	_____
_____	_____	_____
_____	_____	_____
_____	_____	_____
_____	_____	

2 What characteristics of God inspire each of these gestures of worship?

_____

_____

_____

_____

_____

3 Romans 12:1–3 speaks of the body and the mind. How can your body aid your mind in worship?

_____

_____

_____

_____

_____

Day 5

Read Psalm 134.

1 Find as many references as you can to the body, its parts or position. How are these used in prayer or worship?

Body Part	Refer-ence	How Used
_____	_____	_____
_____	_____	_____
_____	_____	_____
_____	_____	_____
_____	_____	_____

2 What characteristics of God inspire each of these gestures of worship?

_____

_____

_____

_____

_____

3 Romans 12:1–3 speaks of the body and the mind. How can your body aid your mind in worship?

_____

_____

_____

_____

Week 25 A New Song

Do you sometimes wake up with a song buzzing through your head, almost as if it had been sitting there all night, waiting to burst out? Maybe it's a song you've heard, or maybe one you hardly remember, so you fill in your own words as you hum, or maybe it's a new song—all yours.

Day 1

Read Psalm 33.

1 What can you imagine of the situations in which the psalmist sings a new song?

_____

_____

2 What praise does the psalmist offer God in his new song?

_____

_____

_____

Day 2

Read Psalm 144.

3 How does he describe God's power?

_____

_____

4 What does he request in his new song?

_____

_____

_____

Day 3

Read Psalm 149.

5 In what different ways are the people told to praise God?

_____

_____

Day 4

Read Revelation 4–5.

6 In Revelation 4–5, the creatures of heaven praise Jesus with five new songs. Find their songs and write out the words.

_____

_____

_____

_____

_____

_____

_____

_____

_____

_____

_____

7 What do these songs tell about Jesus?

_____

_____

_____

8 What emotions are present in these chapters of Revelation?

_____

_____

9 Tell Jesus how it makes you feel to have him living in you. Make some notes here.

_____

_____

_____

Day 5

10 Pick out one of the new songs in these passages. Try to sense the mood of the words. Then make up a tune that fits the words and the mood. Use it as your new song to the Lord. If you're able to do so, write your tune on the staff paper below.

Week 26 Creative Good Works

Day 1

What did you do with your time last week? Disregard the time you spent with "have to" things like eating, sleeping, and school or work. How did you spend the rest of your time? Try making a list with an estimated number of hours for general categories like TV, sports, study, loafing, reading, and music. Need a category for "can't remember"? **Read Ephesians 2:8–10** to discover one of God's reasons for creating new life in you. Now go back over your schedule. How much of what you did last week could be called "good works"?

Things I Did	*How Much Time?*	*Good Works?*

Day 2

Read Titus 1–3 for the next four days.

1 The Book of Titus is a letter from Paul to the young pastor of the new churches on the island of Crete. In what general areas does Paul give advice to Titus?

_____

_____

_____

2 What does Paul say that Titus ought to be teaching his congregations?

_____

_____

_____

Day 3

3 Find six references to good deeds in this book.

_____

_____

4 In view of Paul's broad range of teaching, what would you expect to be included in his definition of good deeds?

_____

_____

_____

5 What part in a believer's life should good deeds have?

_____

_____

Day 4

6 Paul says in Titus 2:14 that Christ's people ought to be "eager to do what is good." How can you cultivate an eagerness for good works?

_____

_____

7 What activities (that could be called good works) do you enjoy so much that you could become *eager* to do them?

_____

_____

Day 5

8 Look again at last week's schedule. Put a check mark next to those activities that work toward making you a better person, helping someone else, or building up God's kingdom. Do you have some extra time left that you could have used for good deeds?

During the next few days, express your thanksgiving to God for new life by setting aside some time to work for him. Let these tasks be part of your worship. Record them below.

Date   *Time*   *Project*

———— ———— ————————————————————————

———— ———— ————————————————————————

———— ———— ————————————————————————

———— ———— ————————————————————————

7 History's Hieroglyphics

Those crazy Israeli!
  On again
  Off again.
Chosen by God,
  yet fickle
Yell for God
  in a jam.
Forget God
  until the next crisis,
And wonder why
  God doesn't bounce
  around to rescue.
They've got God pegged
  all wrong.
But who can peg God?
  Can you?
  Can I?
And if we could,
  would we dare yell for help
  at all?

Ancient Egyptians designed a special kind of writing—a writing in pictures called hieroglyphics. Remnants of this writing still turn up on ancient stones found at archaeological digs. In hieroglyphics, cryptic symbols stood for words whose meaning or sound resembled the picture. It was an ancient game of charades played out with stylus on stone. And it worked. In an era when written language was new, those picture symbols stuck in the mind. And reading and remembering went hand in hand.

History in the Bible carries some of that same advantage. We can read long convoluted lectures from an apostle or a prophet and get lost in the intricate logic. But history is a story. It has time and place and events and people: picture writing. It sticks in our minds.

For the next nine weeks you will study a quick overview of the history of God's people. The focus is primarily on worship—since that's what a "quiet time" is all about. But it is a *history* of worship. How people did it right—and wrong. What happened when worship failed, or succeeded. And what kind of God is sovereign over all the universe, yet invites, even desires, worship from individual people.

You'll open with an experience of Isaiah, a prophet to ancient Judah. Astounding as it may seem, Isaiah saw God. And for him, worship was no problem. It came automatically.

After that you'll begin this picture of history appropriately in Genesis with Abraham, founder of God's chosen people. From there, you'll hop/skip, touching down at dramatic moments all the way to the Apostle Paul's letter to his young friend Timothy nearly two thousand years later.

Enjoy your brief trip through history's hieroglyphics. Let its picture writing cling to your mind—and inspire you to worship.

Week 27 God Is Holy

The country of Judah appeared to be prospering under King Uzziah. He had an army of 307,500 strong men, so neighboring countries treated them with respect. But the Judeans became proud. Who needed God when they had so much power of their own? So God sent Isaiah to warn his people. As if to give the prophet an extra push, God allowed him to see a glimpse of himself. Isaiah tells us what he saw in his sixth chapter.

If we are to worship God, we must know something of what he is like. What does it mean to say that God is holy? Read this chapter every day, and record a few new answers each time.

Read Isaiah 6.

Day 1

1 Suppose you had stood in Isaiah's shoes during the events of verses 1–4. What would your five senses have revealed to you?

_____

_____

2 What qualities in God does this picture suggest?

_____

_____

Day 2

3 How did the seraphim show honor to God?

_____

4 What was Isaiah's reaction to this revelation of God's holiness?

_____

Day 3

5 How did God prepare him for his task of prophesying to the people of Judah?

_____

_____

6 What does the contrast of verses 5 and 8 tell you about the change in Isaiah?

_____

_____

Day 4

7 What was going to be hard about Isaiah's job?

_____

_____

8 From the text finish this sentence about the future of Judah in as many ways as you can. It will be so bad that . . .

_____

_____

_____

_____

Day 5

9 Write the song of the seraphim (3).

_____

_____

What does it tell you about God's nature, power, resources, and scope of dominion? (Look up *holy* in the dictionary.)

_____

_____

Close your eyes and meditate on this song. Worship God for the qualities that it brings to mind.

Week 28 God's Covenant to Abraham

Organized worship started when God called a special group of people to be his own. He began with Abraham, a seventy-five-year-old semi-nomad from Ur. Ur was a city-kingdom of an early Babylonian Empire. The moon-god "Sin" was their chief god. First God called Abraham to travel 600 miles to Haran with relatives, and there his father, Terah, died. Then God called him even farther away from friends and family and those who worshiped false gods.

Although God didn't let Abraham know where he was going, He did reassure him with a covenant. Many times when Abraham was in a difficult situation, God gave his promises again.

This week, you will read about four of the times that Abraham's covenant was given. If you would like to read all of Abraham's story, read all of Genesis 12–25.

Read Genesis 12:1–9; 15:1–21; 17:1–21; 22:1–19.

Day 1

1 Make a chart of God's promises to Abraham. List each promise on the side. Then √ where each promise is recorded.

Promise	Genesis 12:1–9	Genesis 15:1–21	Genesis 17:1–21	Genesis 22:1–19

Day 2

2 What did God repeat each time he talked to Abraham?

_____

_____

What did he add?

_____

_____

_____

3 What does this tell you about God's response to continued worship and obedience?

_____

_____

Day 3

4 What did it cost Abraham to worship God?

_____

_____

Day 4

5 What importance did God place on Abraham's worship?

_____

_____

6 God called Abraham to found a nation of God-worshipers—separate from others. Why would this have been difficult in Ur or Haran?

_____

_____

Day 5

7 As circumcision separated Abraham and his descendants from non-covenant peoples, how does true worship separate you from nonbelievers?

_____

_____

_____

8 What are your regrets about this separation?

_____

_____

9 How has God rewarded your trusting belief?

_____

_____

Pray, thanking God for calling *you* to worship him. Be honest in telling him about your regrets. Thank him for the rewards.

Week 29 Escape

Read again Genesis 15:13–14. God's prophecy came true. Abraham's grand-son, Jacob, and his family of seventy went to Egypt to keep from starving during a famine in Canaan. Joseph saw that they were given good land in Egypt.

But a new king who didn't know Joseph came to power, and eventually the descendants of Abraham became slaves. They were forced to build the pyra-mids that still stand in that country.

Because there were so many Israelites now, the Egyptians began to be afraid and ordered the boy babies killed. But God spared Moses. The 400 years were almost finished, and he was ready to bring his people back to the land he had promised Abraham. Again they would be free to worship him.

Read Exodus 13:17–15:21.

Day 1

1 What reasons can you give for God's leading the people across the sea rather than around it?

---

2 How was Moses' reaction to crisis different from his people's (14:10–14)?

Day 2

3 In what specific ways did God protect his people?

---

4 What changes do you see in the people when you contrast 14:11–12 with 14:31?

Day 3

5 Moses led his people in worship by singing a song to the Lord. Make a list of what he says God has done.

_____

_____

_____

6 Make another list of his descriptions of God.

_____

_____

Day 4

7 Now make a list of what God has done for you. Be specific—Moses was.

_____

_____

_____

Day 5

8 What characteristics of God do you enjoy?

_____

_____

Pray, praising and thanking God for these.

Week 30 The Promised Land

Forty years have passed. Now the glory of God dwells in the Ark of the Covenant instead of in the pillar of fire and the cloud. Moses led his people right up to the border of the Promised Land. But they were afraid of the other tribes living there.

God did not force them to go in, but instead he made them wait in the wilderness until a new generation was born. Then, with only Caleb and Joshua remaining of the people who had crossed the Red Sea, the time again came to enter Canaan.

Read Joshua 3–4.

Day 1

1 How was the experience of crossing the Jordan similar to crossing the Red Sea?

_____

_____

2 How was it different?

_____

_____

_____

Day 2

3 How did Joshua and his people show honor to God?

_____

4 How did God bring glory to himself?

_____

_____

Day 3

5 What was the purpose of the two piles of twelve stones?

_____

_____

Day 4

6 Part of worship is telling our children of times when God has revealed his greatness to us. What kind of "stones" have your parents told you about?

_____

_____

_____

7 What kind of "stones" are you setting up to help you remember your own good times with God?

_____

_____

_____

Day 5

8 This week, create a craft object, painting, or a poem or other writing that will help you remember one of those victorious times. Write your plans or draw your sketch here.

Week 31 Punishment

Six centuries have passed. Israel, with God's help, has conquered the land of Canaan. But there has been a civil split. Now only the tribe of Judah even pretends interest in worshiping God. God gave them their promised land. He gave them judges, prophets, priests, and kings. Isaiah prophesied destruction because of the people's lack of pure worship. They had repented, and God spared Jerusalem from a vicious Assyrian invasion. But that was a hundred years ago, and the people have forgotten their repentance.

Now God sends the prophet Ezekiel, and, with the Babylonian armies bearing down, this time there will be no escape. Let's see what the religious leaders are doing.

Every Day

Pray every day this week for a different leader in your church. Pray especially that God will help that person grow spiritually and that he will protect him or her from false beliefs.

Day	Name
Monday	_____
Tuesday	_____
Wednesday	_____
Thursday	_____
Friday	_____

Read Ezekiel 8–11.

Day 1

1 Read all of Ezekiel's vision (the four chapters) at one sitting. How does it make you feel about God?

_____

Day 2

2 Find four examples of false worship in chapter 8.

_____

_____

_____

How were religious leaders involved in them?

_____

_____

Day 3

3 What was the function of the man with the writing case?

_____

4 In the upcoming battle, would God be on the side of the Babylonian army or the Judean army? Why?

_____

_____

Day 4

5 Find evidence in these chapters of God's glory,

_____

_____

of his wrath,

_____

_____

and of his mercy.

_____

Day 5

6 What importance does God attach to the spiritual conditions of religious leaders?

_____

_____

Week 32 Back Home Again

About seventy years passed. The people of Judah were scattered, as God had said. Many died. Their city and temple were destroyed. But the Babylonian empire was nearing its end. King Cyrus of Persia conquered Babylon in 539 B.C., and Cyrus allowed what was left of the Jewish people to return to Jerusalem. A group of 42,360 came back. Had they repented? Were they quick to rebuild their temple and begin worshiping God again? After many years without religious liberty, what would they do with it now?

Nineteen years *after* their return, the prophet Haggai had something to say.

Read Haggai 1–2.

Day 1

1 God spoke to his people through Haggai four times. When was each message given? What did each one contain?

Message #1: _____

_____

_____

_____

Message #2: _____

_____

_____

_____

Message #3: _____

_____

_____

_____

Message #4: _____

_____

_____

_____

Day 2

2 What was the first concern of the people when they returned home?

_____

3 What happened to their work? Why?

_____

4 What does this tell you about God? His power?

_____

his interests?

_____

his standards for his people?

_____

Day 3

5 God reminds them of his promise (2:5). Read it again in Genesis 17:1–8 and Exodus 29:45–46. (The Exodus promise was given three months after crossing the Red Sea.) What methods had God used to keep his promise?

_____

_____

Day 4

6 What value does God place on receiving true worship from his people?

_____

7 What projects are you likely to put ahead of worshiping God?

_____

Day 5

8 What distractions are you letting hinder your worship?

As you pray today focus your mind on God. Ask his help in overcoming these obstacles.

Week 33 Confident Worship

The book of Hebrews was written to Jewish people who had become Christian believers. They loved their old faith—and their new one. Hebrews discusses the Jewish tradition and Law and shows how Christianity grows out of it. This week we will study a small section that deals with right worship. If you want to learn more about this book that ties the two Testaments together, read Hebrews, beginning to end.

Read Hebrews 10:19–25.

Day 1

1 What is the basis for our worship now?

_____

2 How is our conscience an aid to worship?

_____

_____

Day 2

3 What part do faith, hope, and love play in worship?

_____

_____

_____

Day 3

4 What responsibility do we have for each other as a part of worship?

_____

_____

_____

Day 4

5 What kind of encouragement do you need when you think of Christ's return (25)?

_____

_____

6 What kind of encouragement can you give someone else?

_____

_____

Day 5

7 In view of the value that God places on worship, what attitudes about church attendance and quiet time do you need to change?

_____

_____

8 Wrong attitudes are hard to change. Pray this week that God will help you with these; but you can begin his work by changing the related *actions* yourself. Write about one particular action that you will work on.

_____

_____

Week 34 Practical Advice on Worship

The apostle Paul was in prison at Rome. Soon he would be executed. No one had supported him at his trial. Most of his friends had left. Only the doctor, Luke, stayed with him.

Paul was concerned about all the churches he had started. They were full of new believers, not used to distinguishing between true and false religion. And there were many false teachers. Would the believers become confused and stray away? Paul wrote to his young pastor friend, Timothy, with some final advice.

Read 2 Timothy 1—4.

Day 1

1 Read the entire book at one sitting. Try to picture the writer. What do you see?

_____

_____

Day 2

2 How does Paul build Timothy's confidence (1:3—2:13)?

_____

_____

_____

Day 3

3 What does he warn Timothy to avoid (2:14—26)? Why?

_____

_____

_____

4 What characterizes false religion (1:14–19)?

_____

_____

those who preach it?

_____

those they convert (3:1–9)?

_____

_____

Day 4

5 What is Timothy's defense against false teaching (3:10–17)?

_____

_____

6 What special danger is there in teachers who tell you only what you want to hear (4:1–5)?

_____

Day 5

7 What false teachings have you been exposed to?

_____

8 How are you building resistance against these?

_____

Pray that God will keep you from being a weak person who succumbs to these teachings. Pray that he will help you seek out teachers who speak the truth, whether or not they make you feel comfortable.

Week 35 Worship with the Psalms

The psalmists give us many examples of true worship. Select one of the psalms below for each day of next week. Read it several times. Meditate on it. Record answers to the questions. Use it as a prayer. (You may need to make minor wording changes as you pray the psalm.)

Day 1

Read Psalm 25.

1 How does this psalm describe God?

_____

_____

2 What does it say about me?

_____

_____

3 What am I asking God to do?

_____

_____

_____

_____

4 What promises am I making to him?

_____

_____

Day 2

Read Psalm 27.

1 How does this psalm describe God?

_____

_____

2 What does it say about me?

_____

3 What am I asking God to do?

_____

_____

4 What promises am I making to him?

_____

_____

Day 3

Read Psalm 34.

1 How does this psalm describe God?

_____

_____

2 What does it say about me?

_____

_____

_____

3 What am I asking God to do?

_____

4 What promises am I making to him?

_____

Day 4

Read Psalm 86.

1 How does this psalm describe God?

_____

_____

_____

2 What does it say about me?

_____

_____

3 What am I asking God to do?

_____

_____

_____

4 What promises am I making to him?

_____

_____

Day 5

Read Psalm 103.

1 How does this psalm describe God?

_____

_____

_____

2 What does it say about me?

_____

_____

3 What am I asking God to do?

_____

_____

4 What promises am I making to him?

_____

_____

8 Got the Message? Live It Out!

If you've traveled this far in this studyguide, you've figured out that the Christian faith is no passive system of beliefs for egg-heads huddled over their fine-print expositions of Greek and Hebrew texts. Sure, Christianity needs its scholars. But even scholars must eventually lift their heads (and their bodies) and go out into the real world. When they do, they find that Christian beliefs don't just rest in the brain. If they are beliefs at all, they touch every part of life.

We must live out these beliefs in the way we address a boss who makes sexually harassing remarks, in the way we respond to a fellow student who needs help—now—at the most inopportune time, in the way we react to ridicule when we talk about our faith, and our audience rejects the message—along with the messenger, in the way we keep-on-keeping-on in that faith, even if outward signs say, "You're a naive, gullible chump; if your God is real, he certainly keeps himself in hiding."

During the next four weeks you'll look at some of the Scriptures that help us "live it out!" Whether you're a comfortable scholar or a hands-on performer, you'll find that faith in God, if it is real, will pervade all of life.

Week 36 Faith during Hard Times

The setting is fifth century B.C., Judah. The Israelites had experienced spiritual revival under King Josiah. But now Josiah is dead and his two sons, in rapid succession, had become king. But the people turned away from God. Furthermore, they were threatened by hostile empires around them: Egypt to the south, Babylon to the east. But the political threats didn't cause them to turn to God. Instead the people seemed to be saying, "Grab it all now; it won't last long." In that latter phrase, they were terribly correct.

Day 1

Read Habakkuk 1:1–4.

1 What is Habakkuk's complaint?

_____

_____

2 In view of his prayer, what would you expect to experience in Judah if you lived there?

_____

_____

3 What would you want God to do?

_____

_____

Day 2

Read Habakkuk 1:5–11.

4 Do you think this is the kind of answer Habakkuk expected form God? Why, or why not?

_____

_____

5 How was life in Judah likely to change if God carried out this threat?

_____

_____

6 Why might it be hard to maintain faith in God during the crisis described here?

_____

_____

Day 3

Read Habakkuk 1:12–2:1.

7 How might Habakkuk's description of God in this, his second prayer, help him endure the kind of trauma described in the previous section?

_____

_____

8 Write out three of the phrases Habakkuk uses here to describe God. Meditate on them for a few moments. (Try repeating them quietly several times as a praise to God.) If you truly believed that these words accurately describe God, how might they help you through a personal crisis?

_____

_____

_____

9 Look again at Habakkuk 2:1. What does Habakkuk's plan of action suggest of his inner attitude toward God?

_____

_____

Day 4

Read Habakkuk 2:2–20.

10 Notice the five repetitions of the phrase, "Woe to him . . ." (6, 9, 12, 15, 19). What had the people of Judah done that deserved these judgments?

_____

_____

_____

_____

11 What does this chapter say that confirms God's authority over all of life?

_____

_____

12 How would you feel if you were a prophet with this message?

_____

_____

Day 5

Read Habakkuk 3:1–19.

13 What pictures come to your mind as Habakkuk describes the destruction he expects God to bring on his land?

_____

_____

_____

_____

14 How do even these word pictures of destruction inspire worship?.

_____

_____

15 Read several times Habakkuk's words in verses 17–19. Why would it be hard for Habakkuk, knowing what he knows of the future, to pray these words?

_____

16 How can his prayer become a model for your own faithfulness to God?

_____

_____

_____

17 Try using the pattern of Habakkuk's prayer in verses 17–19 to make your own prayer of faithfulness to God. Substitute some of your own fears of tragedy, for the fig tree buds and grapes on the vine of verse 17. Then pray Habakkuk's ending.

_____

_____

_____

_____

_____

_____

_____

_____

Week 37 Repentance

King David was a "man after God's own heart." The New Testament describes him that way. But he would have also ranked high on any vice squad hit list. How can we reconcile the two? Are God's standards lower than those of the vice squad? No, they are infinitely higher. But God provides ways for relationship to continue, even when those he loves fall short of meeting those demands. God's moral standards are high. But if we fail to reach them, God invites repentance. It's his way of helping us to keep faith and live it out.

Day 1

Read 2 Samuel 11:1–13.

1 What did David do wrong?

_____

2 What complications arose out of that original wrong-doing?

_____

_____

Day 2

Read 2 Samuel 11:14–27.

3 How did David compound his original sin?

_____

4 What other people were affected by David's sin? How?

_____

_____

5 Read again the last statement of this chapter. In addition to the human losses resulting from David's sin, does God's displeasure seem to you a small or a large factor? Why?

_____

_____

_____

Day 3

Read 2 Samuel 12:1–25.

6 How did God demonstrate his hatred of David's sin?

_____

_____

7 How did David demonstrate his repentance?

_____

8 What indications do you find that God still loved David?

_____

_____

Day 4

Read Psalm 51.

9 How does David's prayer reflect a concern about his relationship with God?

_____

_____

10 What effects does he expect confession and forgiveness to have on that relationship?

_____

_____

Day 5

Read Psalm 32.

11 What contrasts does David express in his condition before confession and forgiveness, and afterward?

Before   *After*

_____   _____

_____   _____

12 What responsibilities did David take on as a result of his restored relationship with God?

_____

_____

13 Read Psalm 139:23–24:
"Search me, O God, and know my heart;
Try me and know my anxious thoughts;
And see if there be any hurtful way in me,
And lead me in the everlasting way" (NASB).

Pray these verses. Now wait for God to bring sins to your mind. Ask his forgiveness and help in turning from these sins. Then believe that God has forgiven and cleansed you. Enjoy this, and express to God your thanksgiving.

Week 38 Freedom & Responsibility

Right in the middle of an epistle whose theme is Christian freedom comes a little paragraph on responsibility. In the first few chapters of Galatians, the apostle Paul has been going on and on about not tying ourselves uselessly to laws, not putting unnecessary restrictions on our fellow Christians. "You were called to be *free*," he says. Then without taking a breath, he adds, now "*serve* one another."

From there he goes on to talk about the sinful nature. (We're supposed to fight it.) It seems that Christian freedom doesn't mean freedom to sin. And that leads to one of the loftiest statements in Scripture: a description of the fruit of the Spirit.

And all this in the context of freedom! Part of living out our faith means turning from sin (as David did), but also an inner growing of those nine God-breathed qualities: the fruits of the Spirit.

Every Day

Make a poster or large sign at the beginning of the week listing the nine fruits of the Spirit in Galatians 5:22–23. Each day for nine days, select a "fruit of the day." Write a definition for that fruit. Try in each situation you meet during the day to demonstrate that fruit.

Day 1

Read Galatians 5:13–15.

1 How might an overemphasis on personal freedom pose a threat to Christian unity?

_____

_____

2 What problems have you caused people when you became obsessed with your own rights to freedom?

_____

_____

_____

3 Talk to God about this. If it seems appropriate, take one step today toward healing those problems. Write your intention here.

_____

_____

Day 2

Read Galatians 5:16–21.

4 What natural conflict does Paul outline?

_____

_____

5 What evidences in a person's life would indicate that the sinful nature is gaining control?

_____

_____

Day 3

6 Which of the sins mentioned in verses 19–21 do you have little trouble with?

_____

_____

7 Which have plagued you in the last month?

_____

_____

8 Open yourself to God and ask him to enter your being and take over these areas still governed by your sinful nature. Our sinful nature has great power, so be ready to turn these areas over to him again tomorrow and next week. But perhaps by next month those sensitive areas will be less of a problem.

_____

_____

Day 4

Read Galatians 5:22–25.

9 God does not take away our sinful nature and leave a vacuum. Instead he fills that void with the fruit of the Spirit. What opposites do you find in the list of the Spirit's fruit and the list of the acts of the sinful nature?

_____

_____

_____   _____

10 What benefits have you noticed as you have tried to live out this fruit?

_____

_____

_____

Day 5

Read again Galatians 5:13–26.

11 Notice especially the first and last verse of this section. How would obeying the instructions in between these verses improve relationships between Christians?

_____

_____

_____

12 Bring to mind one relationship between you and another Christian or group of Christians that needs healing. What steps can you take to begin that healing by following the teachings of this passage?

_____

_____

_____

Pray, asking God to cover that relationship with his own perfect nature and to allow you, even with your own imperfections, to be his instrument of reconciliation.

Week 39 Reaching Out

Can we live the Christian faith in isolation? Can we read our Bibles, pray to God, attend our churches, work for Christian organizations, attend Christian schools, and in short, organize our lives in such a way that we avoid any intimate contact with non-Christians?

It sounds warm and loving and unstressful, but it falls short of scriptural commands in both Old and New Testaments. A necessary ingredient of the Christian faith is that it must reach out. It goes with the territory. A faith that locks itself in a religious ghetto, is less than a full-blown living, growing faith.

The prophet Jonah didn't like that aspect of God's plan. It's not that he minded sharing the faith, but he really preferred to choose his own audience. Something, however, went drastically wrong with that plan.

Day 1

Read Jonah 1.

1 How were Jonah's purposes and God's purposes in conflict?

_____

2 What all could the sailors know about God from their experience with Jonah?

_____

_____

3 Look again at verse 17. If you had been Jonah in that situation, what would you have said to God?

_____

_____

_____

Day 2

Read Jonah 2.

4 What do you think was the purpose of the large fish?

5 What words and phrases here show that Jonah knew he was in trouble?

_____

_____

_____

6 Look again at Jonah 1:1–3. What information in chapter two shows that Jonah had a change of heart?

_____

_____

Day 3

Read Jonah 3.
Note: Nineveh was the capital city of Assyria, an enemy neighbor northeast of Israel.

7 What evidence do you see that Jonah did a thorough job of presenting God's message to Nineveh?

_____

_____

8 How did Nineveh exhibit repentance?

_____

_____

_____

9 Do you think Jonah would be pleased or displeased with the results of his ministry? Why?

_____

_____

Day 4

Read Jonah 4.

10 Why had Jonah at first refused to go to Nineveh?

_____

_____

11 Why was Jonah more concerned about the vine than he was about Nineveh?

_____

12 How did God exhibit love both to Jonah and to Nineveh? (Draw your answers from the whole book.)

_____

_____

_____

Day 5

Read Matthew 28:16–20.

13 What similarities do you see between the job God gave to Jonah and the one he gives to New Testament believers?

_____

_____

14 How is this command from Jesus even bigger than Jonah's task?

_____

_____

15 What objections might today's Christians have to that job?

_____

_____

16 How might these two passages help you overcome your hesitations to live out your faith in a way that "makes disciples" for Jesus?

_____

_____

_____

9 Beyond Mushroom Mentality

August 6, 1945. A mushroom cloud hovered over one city in Japan. Three days later, it happened again. And ever since that date every person alert to twentieth-century technology carries that same mushroom cloud in the back of his or her mind. On a moment's notice, it could hover over his own home. And life—if it continued—would never be the same.

Yet, more than a generation has passed since 1945. The mushroom cloud appears only on test sites—increasingly numerous. Children in 1945 have grown, married, birthed children, all the while wondering, "Is my baby the last generation? Or the next to last?"

Because they hear no answer, they put aside money for college knowing that the hundred-year-old college of their choice may vaporize next week. And life goes on—at its routine pace. So far, the mushroom cloud hovers only in the mind.

How should Christians deal with this uncertain future? We are not immune to its threat. Christians collect ulcers and colitis and migraines like the rest of the world's population. But though atomic warfare did not threaten the ancient world, the Scripture is not silent on the subject of an uncertain future. We can draw strength there, for God will teach us how to live, even under the threat of the mushroom cloud.

Week 40 A Bleak Future

Suppose you've had the great fortune of getting in on the ground floor with the man who promises to be the biggest political giant of the decade. He was small potatoes when you first met him, but you see big things in the future. You quit your job, leave your family, pack a small suitcase, and spend two years as his aide. First you just follow him around, but soon he takes you into his confidence. He talks to the crowds in generalities, but for you he explains the deeper meanings behind his theories. You become friends. In time, even the crowds look to you as "one of the leaders." When the time comes, you know you'll ride into power with him.

Then disaster. Your mentor is arrested, convicted of crime, and executed—all in a matter of days. Your own future? Uncertain at best. And what little you can see doesn't look good.

It happened to the followers of Jesus. But even though he died, Jesus didn't leave them alone.

Read Luke 24 every day this week.

Day 1

1 What uncertainties about the future did the followers of Jesus face?

_____

_____

_____

2 If you could have listened in on the conversation described in verse 14, what phrases do you think you would have picked up?

_____

_____

_____

3 Why do you think Jesus' followers did not recognize him at first?

_____

_____

Day 2

4 What steps did Jesus take in revealing himself to them?

_____

_____

_____

5 How might this slow recognition benefit these men?

_____

_____

Day 3

6 Find as many references as you can to the Scriptures in this chapter. In what ways did Jesus emphasize the importance of Scripture?

_____

_____

7 What would it mean to the followers of Jesus that he opened their minds to understand the Scriptures?

_____

_____

8 In what ways has God opened your mind to the Scriptures?

_____

_____

9 What specific responsibilities do you think God gives you because of that increased understanding?

_____

_____

Day 4

10 Look again at your answers to question 1. In what ways were Christ's actions a response to the uncertain feelings of his followers?

_____

_____

_____

11 As they looked back at this crisis point in their faith, what touchstones would they claim as reasons to continue believing?

_____

_____

Day 5

12 Read again verses 46–49. What responsibilities did Jesus give his followers?

_____

13 How might this assignment decrease their apprehension about the future?

_____

_____

14 Read Luke 24 once more. As you review the way Jesus dealt with the fears of his followers about the future and the way he deals with your fears, what similarities can you find? Thank him for these.

_____

_____

Week 41 The Comforter with Us

When Jesus left his disciples and went back to his Father in heaven, he did not leave his followers alone, even then. He gave them the Holy Spirit—that person of the three-part God who lives inside all believers.

Many Christians feel a little uncertain about the Holy Spirit. It's unnerving to know that someone you can't see and don't know very well lives inside you. Then there's the whole area of Holy Spirit power. (Is it like a huge motor with no on-off switch?) And spiritual gifts. (Will I speak in tongues whether I want to or not?) Besides, the Bible doesn't say nearly as much about the Holy Spirit as it does about Jesus and the Father God. So we have every reason to feel uneasy about the Holy Spirit.

Yet, Jesus promised the Holy Spirit as a *Comforter* to help his followers through an uncertain future. In the age of the mushroom cloud, we need him more than ever.

Day 1

Read Romans 8:1–17.

1 In your Bible, circle the phrase "Spirit of ———" each time it appears. What do these names for the Holy Spirit tell about his character?

_____

_____

_____

2 What reasons do you find here for letting the Holy Spirit invade your life?

_____

_____

3 Why might you hesitate to let God have that kind of control?

_____

_____

Day 2

4 What all does it mean to be God's child? (See verses 12–17.)

_____

_____

_____

5 How do you feel about having this kind of relationship with Almighty God?

_____

6 Talk to him about it.

_____

_____

_____

Day 3

Read Romans 8:18–27.

7 What evidence do you see around you that creation needs to be "liberated from its bondage to decay" (21, NIV)?

_____

_____

8 What evidence do you see in human beings, that we too need that kind of liberation?

_____

_____

9 What is the nature of hope as it is described here?

_____

_____

10 In what ways does the Holy Spirit bring hope to a flawed world?

_____

_____

Day 4

Read Romans 8:28–39.

11 Look closely at verse 28. Why might this promise help you face an uncertain future with confidence?

_____

_____

12 What conditions are attached to this promise?

_____

13 Notice the sequence of five steps in verses 29–30. How might this add confidence to the hope already given by the Holy Spirit in verses 18–27?

_____

_____

14 Look again at verses 31–39. If you were worried that you were not quite good enough to stay in God's favor, how might these words help you?

_____

_____

_____

Day 5

Read again all of Romans 8.

15 Write a prayer to God the Holy Spirit expressing praise and thanks for the qualities described in this chapter.

_____

_____

_____

_____

_____

16 If you were to wake some night in a cold sweat from a nightmare about the atomic future, what words from this chapter might bring you calming strength?

_____

_____

Week 42 Supporting Each Other

About a year after a new convert has become part of a group of Christians, he makes an astounding discovery: Christians are extraordinarily human. Sure, they are redeemed by Jesus Christ and tied to each other by the bond of his love. But they are also petty and jealous and selfish and, if pushed into a corner, may lie and cheat like anyone else.

The new convert takes a detached look at this motley crew he calls his "brothers and sisters in Christ," and calculates that he could live quite well without them. After all, God isn't limited to church buildings and fellowship groups. God can be found just as easily alone on a mountain top or in your own kitchen for that matter. Why endure the hassle of intimate friendships with Christians, who are otherwise so much like everyone else?

But the Christian faith is no Lone Ranger religion. Intrinsic to this faith is its group nature. Our new life in Christ demands fellowship. It demands living out through the give-and-take of community. It is that family of believers who form an insurance policy of protection against an uncertain future. Several passages of Scripture speak to this. You'll look at some of them this week.

Day 1

Read James 5:13–20.

1 Using the whole passage, in what ways are Christians to be responsible for one another?

_____

_____

_____

2 What different circumstances mentioned here show the way a Christian's response is to be different from other people's?

_____

_____

3 Why are these responses best performed in a group setting?

_____

Day 2

4 In the drama of verses 14–15, what part does each person play?

5 What personality characteristics would an elder need to develop in order to perform this work?

6 What personality qualities would a person need to develop to receive this kind of help?

7 What protection do the instructions here offer a Christian who is tempted to stray from faith?

Day 3

Read Romans 12:1–8.

8 What different meanings does Paul attach to the word *body* in these verses?

9 What effect does each of these meanings have on the way Christians function together?

Day 4

10 Paul has told us that in the body of Christ, "each member belongs to all the others" (5). Using verses 6–8, contrast the way one might use each gift with and without an awareness of this truth.

Gift	How I might use it for my own benefit	How I might use it because it belongs to all the others
_____	_____	_____
_____	_____	_____
_____	_____	_____
_____	_____	_____
_____	_____	_____
_____	_____	_____
_____	_____	_____

11 If you are to take to heart the words of verse 5, what changes should you make in your current relationships with people in your church or fellowship group?

_____

_____

_____

Day 5

Read Psalm 133.

12 What word pictures did David use to describe the unity of God's people?

_____

_____

13 What indications do you see that David considered this unity of great value?

_____

14 If unity between God's people is, in part, an insurance policy for an uncertain future, what groundwork should you be laying now so that, if trouble comes, you can receive help from that policy? (Trouble might come in the form of social, emotional, spiritual, physical, as well as material needs.)

_____

_____

_____

15 What groundwork should you be laying so that you can contribute to it
when someone else is in need?

Week 43 A Glorious Future

Suppose the worst happens. Suppose human beings manage to rise up and kill each other off and, at the same time, make the environment uninhabitable. What then? Is it all over? God's creation charred to nothing? God's people reduced to skeletons and piled along side the rest? Is there any hope in this "worst case" future?

The last two chapters of the Bible say, yes.

Read aloud all of Revelation 21–22 every day.

Every Day

1 Every day tell God something different that you appreciate about the plan he has revealed in these chapters.

Monday_____

Tuesday_____

Wednesday_____

Thursday_____

Friday_____

Day 1

2 How does this passage of Scripture make you feel? Why?

_____

_____

_____

3 Find as many contrasts as you can between the new heaven and earth and what we have now.

Now   *Then*

_____   _____

_____   _____

_____   _____

_____   _____

Day 2

4 What pictures of God's glory do you find in these chapters?

_____

_____

_____

5 What do you see of his love for his people?

_____

_____

_____

Day 3

6 How will the relationship that God has with his people be different from what it is now?

_____

_____

_____

7 Pray today, praising God for some of his qualities revealed in these two chapters.

_____

_____

_____

Day 4

8 What do you find in these two chapters that you will enjoy experiencing?

_____

_____

9 What connections do you find in the character of God, as it is revealed here, and what you have learned about him in your previous studies of Scripture?

_____

_____

_____

Day 5

Read Revelation 21–22 again.

10 What is uncertain about your own future?

_____

_____

_____

11 What, according to these chapters, is certain?

_____

_____

12 How can the pictures presented here help you endure the uncertainties?

_____

_____

_____

10 On-your-own Bible Study

O send thy Spirit, Lord,
Now unto me,
That he may touch mine eyes,
And make me see:
Show me the truth concealed
Within the Word,
And in thy Book revealed
I see the Lord. *

You've been following a devotional guide for nearly a year now. You've formed consistent habits of Bible study and prayer. You've gathered ideas about what to look for in a passage of Scripture. You've learned to pray straight out to God or from his own prayer book, the Psalms. You've become aware that studying Scripture means change in yourself, and the change is sometimes painful. You are growing.

But you can't forever follow a study guide. It's too limited—not aimed just at you. It's time to branch out and do your own study. You're ready for "on-your-own Bible study."

You deserve a mild warning, however. It's not easy. Those hidden meanings don't often leap off the page and scamper into your brain. Soul-searching questions that make you grow don't just happen. It takes work. But it's well worth the effort. And once you get used to seriously studying the Bible, it all comes rather naturally. This final chapter will teach you how to study the Bible inductively.

Inductive Bible study is a method of studying the Bible in much the same way that a scientist studies an unknown chemical. You first read the passage as though you've never seen it before. (Maybe you haven't.) Then, through a series of regular steps, you discover its content and meaning.

During this two-month period, you'll have a chance to study nine passages inductively on your own. The steps of inductive study have been divided into six parts, one for each day. Read 1 Corinthians 15 and follow the study that is done for you. Then refer back to its example as you do your own study of the passages listed for each week. All quotes from the Bible are from the *New American Standard Bible.*

*From "Break Thou the Bread of Life," by Mary A. Lathbury, 1877.

The first section using 1 Corinthians 15 is a sample. After that you'll find blank pages with an outline for your first week's work. For the remaining eight weeks, use a notebook to follow that same outline. But use the passages of Scripture listed in your studyguide. When you've finished that, you are truly "on your own." Happy exploring!

1 Corinthians 15 Sample Study

Day 1: First Glances

A. Once over lightly

1. What comes before?
A chapter about spiritual gifts, particularly tongues and prophecy.

2. After?
A final chapter of personal notes.

3. Author's style?
Logical, orderly.

4. How does it make you feel?
Encouraged, excited, important.

5. Major characters?
God, Christ, Paul the writer, believers.

6. Theme?
Life after death.

7. Conclusions?
God has conquered death. Keep on believing and working for God, because we will live forever with Him (56–58).

B. A closer look

1. Major divisions?
Verses 1–11, 12–19, 20–28, 29–34, 35–50, 51–58.

2. Illustrations?
If Christ was raised, then we also will be raised.

3. Order of events or teachings?
Christ was raised. That's why we believe in him. God has authority over all—even death. Our lives show that we believe Christ was raised. Our new bodies will be better than our old ones. The event of resurrection is described.

4. What can you know about the writer?
He was an apostle; he persecuted the church; he worked hard; Christ appeared
to him; he felt unworthy (8–10); he lived in danger (30).

5. About the people he wrote to?
Believers who needed encouragement.

Day 2: The Big W's (and One H)

1. Who? Describe the characters and their relationships.
Brethren—Paul's readers
Christ—raised, was seen alive, firstfruits, the man of heaven
Cephas—saw the resurrected Christ
500 brethren—same
James—same
Apostles—same
Me (Paul)—Christ also appeared to him
God—has put all things in subjection
The dead—will be raised
Adam—First Adam became a living being; last Adam (Jesus) became a life-
    giving spirit
God's enemies—they will all be put under Christ's feet, last enemy to be de-
    stroyed is death
We—not all sleep, will be changed

2. What happened? List the sequence of events or progress of an idea.
Christ died, was buried, then raised. Many saw his resurrected body. Therefore,
God has conquered death and we, too, will be raised.

3. Where? Use a map. Check distance and geography.
Ephesus—Paul could have fought with beasts there.

4. When? Tell when in history, time of day, year, or season.
Third day—Christ was raised
"When all things are subjected to him then the Son himself also will be sub-
    jected" (28).
"When this perishable will have put on the imperishable . . . DEATH IS SWAL-
    LOWED UP IN VICTORY" (54).

5. Why? Look for the words "because," "for," "when," "since."
"For since by a man came death, by a man resurrection" (21).
"For as in Adam all die, so also in Christ all shall be made alive" (22).

"For he must reign until he has put all his enemies under his feet" (25).
"For this perishable must put on the imperishable" (53).
"Therefore [because of this] be steadfast" (58).

6. How? Note by what process.
"In Christ all shall be made alive. But each in his own order" (22-23).

Day 3: Get the Picture

Studying the Bible can be like working a jigsaw puzzle. It takes a long time if you just keep trying to fish pieces out of the box. Instead, you lay all the pieces out, picture side up. Then you can *see* how it fits together.

There are several ways to lay out the pieces of a Scripture passage. Try *one* of the following on day 3.
1. Outline
2. Write a summary for each paragraph
3. Write your own paraphrase of the passage
4. Give a title to each paragraph
5. Draw a chart—see the chart for 1 Corinthians 15 on the next page.

Day 4 The Nitty-Gritty

One way to discover what a writer intended you to understand is to "get inside" his writing style and see how he put his words and concepts together. The Bible is excellent literature and will stand careful scrutiny. Look for the following elements of writing structure as you study a passage.

1. Repetition
Appeared—verses 5–8
Raised—verses 4, 12, 14, 16, 17, 20, 29, 32, 35, 43
Perishable-imperishable—verses 42, 50, 53–54
Sown—verses 42–44

2. Continuity—repeated use of similar terms
Raised/resurrection
Perishable/mortal
Imperishable/immortality
Fallen asleep/dead

3. Contrast—putting opposites side by side to emphasize their differences
By man came death, by a man comes resurrection (21)
As in Adam all die; in Christ alive

Sown is perishable; raised is imperishable
Sown in dishonor; raised in glory
Sown in weakness; raised in power
Sown in physical body; raised a spiritual body
First man from earth; second from heaven (47)
Dead will be resurrected
Victory accompanies death

4. Comparison—putting similar things together for emphasis
I work harder than any of them (10)
A body and a kernel of wheat (35–38)
The glory of a celestial body and the glory of a terrestrial body (40–41)

Paul's Argument for Life after Death (1 Corinthians 15)

Verse	Reason	Evidence	If it were not true...	Since it's true...
3–20	Jesus raised from the dead	He was seen by many	1) Our preaching and faith are in vain. 2) We are misrepresenting God. 3) You are still in your sins. 4) This life is all there is. The dead are dead forever.	Christ is the first of many who will be raised.
20–28	God has authority over everything, even death	Adam was God's creation. Yet all died because of his sin against God.	Some forces would be more powerful than God.	Everything—even death—is under subjection to God the Father.
29–34	Believers behave as if there is a resurrection.	Baptism. Their dangerous lives. They don't try to get all they can here.	The believers would eat, drink, and not risk their lives.	They must believe in a resurrection or they wouldn't live the way they do.
35–50	We will have new bodies.	In nature, seeds die and produce plants. As our first body was like Adam's, our second will be like Christ's.	Our current bodies wouldn't be suited for heaven.	God will prepare us for life with him.
51–58	Our resurrection will fulfill prophecy.	Isaiah 25:8 Hosea 13:14	We would be under the power of sin and law.	God gives us victory over death.

This glory is like resurrection (42)
First Adam became a living body, last Adam a life-giving Spirit (45)
As we bear image of man of dust, we'll also bear image of man of heaven (49)

5. *General and particulars*
I preached to you the gospel; then note the details of verses 3–11.

Day 5 More Nitty-Gritty

6. *Cause and effect—Look for the words "then," "therefore," "since," and "because"*
"If Christ has not been raised, then our preaching is in vain." (See the other if-thens of 12–19.)
"Therefore . . . be steadfast" (58). This is the effect of all that Paul has said thus far.

7. *Explanation—Look for the words "that," "so that," "in order that"*
"So it is with the resurrection of the dead" (42). (Then look back at 35–41 for the explanation.)

8. *Introduction*
"Now I make known to you, brethren" (1).

9. *Progression—a sequence from least to greatest.*
Christ died, was buried, raised, appeared (3–5)
If there is no resurrection, then (1) Christ was not raised; (2) our preaching is vain; (3) your faith is vain; (4) we are misrepresenting God; (5) you are still in your sins; (6) those who are dead have perished; (7) we all ought to be pitied (12–19)
Christ the firstfruits, then those who belong to him, then the end (23–24)

10. *Questions—write the questions in the passage, then note their answers*
"How do some among you say that there is no resurrection of the dead?" (12)
"Otherwise, what will those do who are baptized for the dead?" (29)
"Why then are they baptized for them?" (29)
"Why are we also in danger every hour?" (30)
"How are the dead raised?" (35)
"With what kind of body do they come?" (35)
"O death, where is your victory?" (55)
"O death, where is your sting?" (55)

Day 6 So What!

You have now completed a very thorough literary analysis of a portion of Scripture. If you had been studying a scene from Shakespeare, you would now be familiar with all its intricacies.

But don't stop. The Bible is not Shakespeare. It is a book to live by. What are you going to do with all the facts and understanding of the past week? God holds us responsible to act on this kind of knowledge. Ask yourself questions like these:

1. Do I believe this?
2. How should my actions show that I believe it?
3. How do I need to change my ideas? values? attitudes? actions?
4. Does this answer a problem I am having?
5. What is God showing me about himself? about my relationship with him?
6. How can I worship God better because of this?
7. What does God want me to do?
8. What does he want me to become?
9. What is God promising me?

Week 44 John 11:1–44

Day 1: First Glances

A. Once over lightly

1 What comes before?

_____

_____

2 After?

_____

_____

3 Author's style?

_____

4 How does it make you feel?

_____

5 Major characters?

_____

_____

6 Theme?

_____

7 Conclusions?

_____

_____

B. A closer look

1 Major divisions?

2 Illustrations?

3 Order of events or teachings?

4 What can you know about the writer?

5 About the people he wrote to?

Day 2: The Big W's (and One H)

1 Who? Describe the characters and their relationships.

2 What happened? List the sequence of events or progress of an idea.

3 Where? Use a map. Check distance and geography.

_____

_____

4 When? Tell when in history, time of day, year, or season.

_____

_____

5 Why? Look for the words "because," "for," "when," "since."

_____

_____

_____

_____

6 How? Note by what process.

_____

_____

_____

Day 3: Get the Picture

Use the next page to do *one* of the following:
1. Outline
2. Write a summary for each paragraph
3. Write your own paraphrase of the passage
4. Give a title to each paragraph
5. Draw a chart

Day 4: The Nitty-gritty

1 Repetition

_____

_____

_____

_____

2 Continuity—repeated use of similar terms

_____

_____

_____

_____

3 Contrast—putting opposites side by side to emphasize their difference

_____

_____

_____

_____

4 Comparison—putting similar things together for emphasis

_____

_____

_____

5 General and particulars

_____

_____

_____

_____

Day 5: More Nitty-gritty

6 Cause and effect—look for the words "then," "therefore," "since," "because."

_____

_____

_____

_____

7 Explanation—look for the words "that," "so that," "in order that."

_____

_____

_____

8 Introduction

_____

9 Progression—a sequence from least to greatest

_____

_____

_____

10 Questions—write the questions in the passage, then note their answers

_____

_____

_____

_____

Day 6: So What!

1 Do I believe this?

_____

2 How should my actions show that I believe it?

_____

_____

_____

3 How do I need to change my ideas?

_____

values?

_____

attitudes?

_____

actions?

_____

4 Does this answer a problem I am having?

_____

_____

_____

5 What is God showing me about himself?

_____

_____

_____

about my relationship with him?

_____

_____

_____

6 How can I worship God better because of this?

_____

_____

_____

7 What does God want me to do?

_____

_____

_____

8 What does he want me to become?

_____

_____

_____

9 What is God promising me?

_____

_____

_____

_____

Weeks 45–52

Now it's your turn. Use the six-day pattern for each of the following Scripture portions using a separate notebook for your quiet time study. Not all the inductive questions will have answers in each passage. But keep digging. You'll be surprised at how much you'll find.

This unit has heavy emphasis on Bible study, but Bible study is only one part of a good quiet time. Don't forget to use part of your time talking to God. He speaks to you through his Word, and he wants you to speak to him in prayer.

Week 45: Matthew 7

Week 46: Colossians 1:1–23

Week 47: 1 Kings 18

Week 48: Joel 1–3

Week 49: Acts 2

Week 50: Psalm 8

Week 51: Proverbs 31

Week 52: 1 Corinthians 13

Prayer Notebook

date	request	date of answer

date	request	date of answer

date   date of answer

Scripture Index

Genesis 1–2 *56*
Genesis 12:1–9 *86*
Genesis 13:1–13 *19*
Genesis 15:1–21 *86*
Genesis 17:1–21 *86*
Genesis 18:16–33 *19*
Genesis 22:1–19 *86*
Exodus 13:17–15:21 *89*
Exodus 26:31–37 *35*
Leviticus 16 *35*
Joshua 3–4 *91*
Judges 6–7 *29*
1 Samuel 1:1–2:10, 21 *10*
1 Samuel 9:25–10:13 *69*
2 Samuel 11:1–12:25 *112–12*
1 Kings 18 *150*
1 Kings 19 *27*
Psalm 1 *31*
Psalm 8 *150*
Psalm 19:7–11 *31*
Psalm 25 *102*
Psalm 27 *102*
Psalm 32 *112*
Psalm 33 *76*
Psalm 34 *103*
Psalm 51 *112*
Psalm 63 *73*
Psalm 86 *104*
Psalm 95 *74*
Psalm 103 *104*
Psalm 104 *60*
Psalm 105 *21*
Psalm 106 *21*
Psalm 119:97–112 *32*
Psalm 133 *129*
Psalm 134 *74*
Psalm 136 *21*
Psalm 139 *58*
Psalm 144 *76*
Psalm 149 *77*
Proverbs 31 *150*
Isaiah 6 *84*
Isaiah 36–37 *13*
Isaiah 42 *61–64*

Ezekiel 8–11 *93*
Joel 1–3 *150*
Jonah 1–4 *117–18*
Habakkuk 1–3 *107–10*
Haggai 1–2 *95*
Matthew 7 *150*
Matthew 26–28 *37*
Matthew 28:16–20 *119*
Mark 10:46–52 *51*
Luke 15:11–32 *16*
Luke 19:1–10 *51*
Luke 24 *121*
John 4:4–42 *51*
John 11:1–44 *142*
John 13:34–35 *53*
John 14:15–31 *69*
Acts 2 *150*
Acts 10:1–11:26 *42*
Romans 6 *65*
Romans 8 *124–26*
Romans 12:1–3 *71*
Romans 12:1–8 *128*
1 Corinthians 13 *150*
1 Corinthians 15 *136–41*
2 Corinthians 5:14–21 *69*
Galatians 5:13–26 *114–16*
Ephesians 2:8–10 *79*
Ephesians 4:1–16 *44*
Ephesians 4:17–32 *70*
Ephesians 5:15–6:4 *49*
Colossians 1:1–23 *150*
1 Timothy 2:1–8 *72*
2 Timothy 3:16–17 *30*
2 Timothy 1–4 *100*
Titus 1–3 *79*
Philemon *47*
Hebrews 1 *25*
Hebrews 4:12 *31*
Hebrews 7:22–10:25 *39*
Hebrews 10:19–25 *98*
James 5:13–20 *127*
1 John 3:11–4:21 *53*
Revelation 4–5 *77*
Revelation 21–22 *131*

Young Fisherman Bible Studyguides

Group studies for students in junior and senior high are used by youth groups, Sunday schools, camps, and Christian school classes. Old Testament, New Testament, and topical studies challenge students to develop a genuinely biblical approach to life as they discover *for themselves* what the Bible teaches. *Features:* humorous illustrations in the student workbook; reduced student page, background material, and notes for each question in the teacher edition.

JOSHUA: Promises to Keep, 13 studies by Roberta Green. student, 433–1; teacher, 434–X

MARK: God on the Move, 16 studies by Carolyn Nystrom. student, 311–4; teacher, 312–2

ACTS 1–12: Church on the Move, 10 studies by Carolyn Nystrom. student, 125–1; teacher, 126–X

ACTS 13–28: Missions Accomplished, 16 studies by Margaret Fromer & Carolyn Nystrom. student, 010–7; teacher, 011–5

ROMANS: Christianity on Trial, 16 studies by Carolyn Nystrom. student, 898–1; teacher, 899–X

GALATIANS: Free at Last, 13 studies by Sandy & Dale Larsen. student, 293–2; teacher, 294–0

PHILIPPIANS: Living Joyfully, 12 studies by Ron Klug. student, 681–4; teacher, 682–2

JAMES: Roadmap for Down-to-Earth Christians, 12 studies by Margaret Fromer & Carolyn Nystrom. student, 419–6; teacher, 420–X

AT THE STARTING LINE: Beginning a New Life, 8 studies by Carolyn Nystrom. student, 053–0; teacher, 054–9

CHOICES: Picking Your Way Through the Ethical Jungle, 12 studies by Sandy & Dale Larsen. student, 113–8; teacher, 114–6

FORGIVENESS: No Guilt, No Grudges, 13 studies by Sandy & Dale Larsen. student, 277–0; teacher, 278–9

GET WISE: Studies in Proverbs, 12 studies by Phil Ackley. student, 695–4; teacher, 696–2

THE REAL QUESTIONS: Searching the Psalms for Answers, 12 studies by Ron Klug. student, 701–2; teacher, 702–0

Personal Bible Studyguides

Daily studies in the New Testament provide just the right balance between discovering truth for yourself and learning from trusted Bible scholars. Each day you will pray, read Scripture, discover meaning through four inductive questions, read commentary notes by Scripture Union authors, keep a journal of your response to God, and work on memorizing a key verse.

MARK: A Daily Dialogue with God, 53 studies by Ron Klug. 539–7

JOHN: A Daily Dialogue with God, 65 studies by Whitney Kuniholm. 431–5

ROMANS: A Daily Dialogue with God, 40 studies by James Reapsome. 731–4

GALATIANS, EPHESIANS, PHILIPPIANS, & COLOSSIANS: A Daily Dialogue with God, 54 studies by Whitney Kuniholm. 292–4

HEBREWS, JAMES, 1 & 2 PETER, JUDE: A Daily Dialogue with God, 56 studies by Dale Larsen. 339–4

Fisherman Bible Studyguides

Inductive Bible studies for student, church, and neighborhood groups include almost 40 Old Testament, New Testament, and topical studies. For a complete list of Fisherman Bible Studyguides, write to Harold Shaw Publishers, Box 567, Wheaton, Illinois 60189.

Carpenter Studyguides
Bible study *plus*, for small groups within the church. Includes worship, prayer, outreach, relationship-building, and more. Groups use members handbooks as well as leaders handbooks containing additional ideas for enhancing the life of the group. For a complete list of Carpenter studyguides, write to Harold Shaw Publishers.

You can learn more about all of the Shaw studyguides by obtaining a *free* **Harold Shaw Publishers BIBLE STUDY CATALOG:** a 32-page illustrated booklet describing each of the nearly 70 studyguides in the Fisherman, Young Fisherman, Carpenter, and Personal Bible Studyguides series. It's a helpful planning tool. Also available is **The Fisherman's Net,** a *free* resource quarterly for Bible study leaders.

All studyguides and materials are available at your local bookstore or from Harold Shaw Publishers, Box 567, Wheaton, Illinois 60189.